Piggy Bank to Credit Card

PIGGY BANK TO CREDIT CARD

TEACH YOUR CHILD THE FINANCIAL FACTS OF LIFE

LINDA BARBANEL

M.S.W., C.S.W.

CROWN TRADE PAPERBACKS, NEW YORK

Copyright © 1994 by Linda Barbanel
Illustrations © by Bryan Hendrix

Published by Crown Publishers, Inc., 201 East 50th Street, New York, New York 10022. Member of the Crown Publishing Group.

Random House, Inc. New York, Toronto, London, Sydney, Auckland

CROWN TRADE PAPERBACK and colophon are trademarks of Crown Publishers, Inc.

Manufactured in the United States of America

Library of Congress Cataloging-in-Publication Data
Barbanel, Linda.
    Piggy bank to credit card: teach your child the financial facts
of life / Linda Barbanel.—1st ed.
        p.   cm.
    Includes bibliographical references and index.
    1. Children—Finance, Personal—Study and teaching.   2. Children's
allowances—Handbooks, manuals, etc.   3. Consumer education—
Handbooks, manuals, etc.   I. Title.
HG179.B297   1994
332.024—dc20   93–14973
                                                                 CIP

ISBN 0–517–88049–0

10 9 8 7 6 5 4 3 2 1

First Edition

This book is dedicated to the remarkably creative and kind people in my writers' group, who listened, critiqued, and encouraged this project. Sincere thanks go to Edith Anderson, Lois H. Arkin, Roz Bloch, Karen Burdick, Vivian Eyre, Livi French, Wendy Glickstein, Susan Kramer, Larry Messin, Carlyn Parker, Dorothy Pierce, Frances Rubinsky, Margaret Scanlon, and Hilda Terry. I am also most grateful to Hannelore Hahn, executive director of the International Women's Writing Guild, who initiated this group with a "Zip Code Party" of writers in my area.

CONTENTS

ACKNOWLEDGMENTS

MANY THANKS GO TO EDYTHEA SELMAN, MY AGENT, WHO believed, when she saw that I was speaking on kids and money, that a book was in me. I truly loved working with Irene Prokop, my editor, whose gentle style helped me put the book into shape. Also, thanks to Joanne Golden, Joann Rosoff, Charles Baxley, and Steven Katz for their helpful comments. If it were not for Todd Lewis and Sandy Fleisher, I would not have gotten to work on the computer as easily. Thanks to Jerry Sieser and Josiah Silverstein for their considerable photographic talents. I am especially grateful to the many writers and media hosts who interviewed me on how kids can learn to manage money. And to my son, Eric, my friends, and so many people across the country whose experiences with money provided me with anecdotes for this book, my sincere thanks.

INTRODUCTION: HOW TO TALK ABOUT MONEY WITH CHILDREN

LEARNING THE NUTS AND BOLTS ABOUT MONEY, INCLUDING planning for expenditures, postponing gratification, and making financial decisions, develops over time. Most of us have imprinted values from years of seeing and experiencing repeated spending patterns and conversations. For many, there is great confusion about the power of money because it can be a taboo topic within the family.

Managing money is something almost all human beings have to do in their lifetime. In our society, handling money involves far more than knowing how much something costs and figuring out a way to get the money we need to have the necessities and niceties of life. Values and attitudes are at the heart of spending, saving, investing, donating, bargain hunting, record keeping, and paying taxes. Whether you are male or female is a factor in how you manage money, since different expectations are learned from parents, television, friends, and teachers. Wishes and worries are also inherent in our fantasies about money, because we often hope it can magically bring what we really need deep inside.

To be mature with money, it is necessary to have a mastery of the facts of financial life together with a comfortable and realistic set of attitudes to guide our behavior. The goal is to be able to use money rather than to abuse it, to have a realistic view of what money can buy, and to be able to talk about it easily and appropriately.

Talking about money with children can be difficult for parents.

It is a subject husbands and wives have enormous difficulty discussing between themselves. As a result, arguing about money is common. If we do not teach our children about money, they will lack the self-esteem that comes with doing meaningful things; they will limit themselves by passing up opportunities they do not understand; they can fall into bad habits that are not only hard to break but may be very expensive emotionally and financially.

Basically, all parents want their children to grow up to become responsible, independent adults. It seems such an irony, then, that so little effort and imagination go into teaching children about the role that money plays in daily life.

Learning the "financial facts of life" involves a certain mastery of the rules of the game which come with different stages of a child's development. The ability to conceive of the abstractions of worth, value, and quality, for example, comes later than those of saving, trading, and sharing.

If you gradually teach children how to handle money in a responsible way, they will be ready for the demands of the adult world. When children have a realistic knowledge that money is for enjoyment as well as for spending and sharing, they will be equipped to use it rather than to abuse it. Your children will feel secure in their daily financial dealings. They will grow more confident of their abilities to manage their money because they feel you have trust in them. The money-savvy adolescent is more independent, more resourceful, and does not expect his parents to pay for everything or satisfy his every consumer whim.

Helping children learn the proper attitudes to guide their monetary behavior so they can enjoy themselves as financially independent beings is the goal of this book. If parents neglect this lesson, children will have no knowledge of the most basic tool of daily life.

Part One

SETTING
THE
FINANCIAL
STAGE

1

THE FIRST YEARS

TALKING ABOUT MONEY CAN BEGIN VERY EARLY. CHILDREN AS young as two or three show curiosity about the way the world works. We need to convey in a warm, simple, and loving way that the subject of money is important.

As you talk about money with your children, there is a good possibility that your own memories, doubts, and fears will surface. It may surprise you that you carry misinformation from your own childhood. Rethinking past experiences can help you understand where childhood perceptions may have been distorted, since what seemed perfectly clear to you as a child often is no longer so with insight and hindsight. Sharing those misperceptions and mistakes with children can be very helpful. This tells your child that it is all right not to "know it all." It also allows the child to laugh with you if those mistakes strike you both as funny. When children are able to talk freely and easily about money, they will talk about other things as well.

Try to keep your eyes and ears open to how your child responds to money subjects. If you sense that there is something in your child's behavior or attitude which needs to be discussed, you can choose the words to suit the situation in a short and simple way that satisfies curiosity—just as you would with sexual questions. Parents who are sensitive to things such as differences in life-style and competitiveness among their children's friends have material for good conversations. That is how values are conveyed. It is also an opportunity to offer support and guidance. Talking can resolve issues before they become problems.

Children are copycats. They pick up parental quirks as they grow and identify with the parent of the same sex. Who pays for the large and small items, who makes the decisions for purchases, who takes care of the nitty-gritty bookkeeping—how these daily chores are handled and the spirit of doing them are subconsciously sponged up by children. Most of what is learned is not spoken; it is copied.

Therefore, mothers and fathers should take a long look at their own financial habits and attitudes. If you and your spouse have totally different ideas about money, you need to rectify your differences to avoid confusing your child. If one parent is in charge of money matters, the other ought to be aware of the details and defer to that parent to eliminate the possibility of sabotage by your spouse and manipulation by your child.

To work on this together, first establish that you both want your child to learn good habits about money; you want peaceful coexistence in your household; you regard sabotage as a serious infraction of your marital relationship. You can recognize each other's limitations and proclivities with money without attacking each other. Focus on understanding your own style to decide who does best with such things as allowances and checkbooks. Try to find areas of agreement. What are your ideas about debt, bailouts, and saving? Can you agree on a modus operandi for handling kids' requests for extra money? Determining these financial guidelines can fend off arguments as well as help you and your spouse set the stage for a healthy environment for your children.

EARLY ANXIETIES

Anxiety is a demon everyone knows. Babies depend on adults to relieve their discomfort and take care of them so they will feel better. When they grow up, they will use what they've learned in order to tolerate their own frustrations and daily stresses. Money can help people to feel better too. For those whose anxiety level is high, spending excessive amounts of money is a favorite release.

Children look to parents for reassurance and soothing to feel more secure. Parents who want to keep their child quiet at all costs pop a pacifier into the child's mouth or feed him at the first sign of discomfort. Later on, the child may continue to get the things he wants simply because the pattern of keeping him quiet was started very early. The child learns to expect gratification at the first twinge of discomfort.

Other parents believe that babies should be left to cry. Long-lasting power struggles can result from this pattern, since it puts the parent in charge of when and how much gratification is received. The child learns that it's too tough, or utterly hopeless, to get what he wants and can give up trying. This attitude can carry over into adulthood in people who lack ambition or are depressed. They may feel unwilling to work hard, since rewards come too late or not at all. To protect themselves, and to feel a sense of control, they might minimize the importance of money. Conversely, an adult who was denied gratification as a child can try to be as independent as possible. Those who provide their own gratification don't have to depend on anyone, and they avoid having to wait and see if others will respond to them.

Yet, none of us had a completely blissful childhood where all our needs were met. Society favors those with money in the bank who are thrifty, self-sufficient, and pay their bills on time. The anxiety of insecurity is translated into security-oriented behavior such as saving for a rainy day, bargain hunting to prove one's ability to survive in this tough world by being able to stretch dollars, denying oneself material goods, or turning toward collecting valuable things. These types of behavior are all socially acceptable and are motivated by fears which we all have to some extent.

FEEDING PATTERNS

Feeding in infancy can also influence later behavior with money. The old-fashioned idea about building character by feeding babies on a rigid schedule is an example. This style of feeding makes babies angry at the care giver rather than enabling them to develop patience and the need for delayed gratification. We see this later on when money becomes a nurturing substance, and we all know people who have voracious appetites for consumer products.

Even the words in our language for money have elements reminiscent of this earliest feeding stage. When food and money are both felt to be essential to survival, such words as *lettuce*, *bread*, and *dough* are used. The term *money hungry* implies the need for repetitive monetary replenishment and an overeagerness to get the necessary supply, as if existence itself hinged on having money.

In extreme cases where children do not get enough food, they worry that there will never be enough money either. The most insecure people behave like squirrels when they get older, putting away their money and living frugally so they will never be caught short. They worry about the "rainy day" when they will need their accumulated money and resent mightily having to dig into it at all, even for essentials. Money is their security from being a have-not.

Money also acts as a substitute for the feelings of contentment experienced after a meal, when the stomach is full. For those people who lived through the Depression, for example, there may be memories of hunger pangs. These people feel drained and depleted without money, as if their life fluids and energy hinged solely on their money supply.

Children who experience discomfort from being hungry, or not digesting food properly, may learn to expect that food will cause pain. Later, they may have the attitude that life is difficult. Attitudes toward life and money develop according to what the earliest experiences are, how physical functioning progresses, and what feelings are generated in the feeder and the fed.

As the baby grows and can feed himself, some new challenges occur. Mom's desire for a clean kitchen may conflict with baby's need to play with his food. Children can be very sloppy with money, too. This is also a situation that needs to be tolerated for a while. Just as with food, children have to throw money around before they learn to handle it more adroitly.

Some parents try hard to make sure their child has a stress-free environment. They put too many toys within the child's reach or feed the child before he signals he's hungry. These parents take over the child's responsibilities, and the child loses the chance to gain esteem from doing the job himself, getting to know his own feelings, or finding a way to tolerate small amounts of frustration.

TOILET TRAINING AND POWER

Consider what happens in the second year of life when toilet training usually takes place. The battle of the potty pits Mom against babe. Babies don't like demands and can fight them by not "giving." This stance can be seen later when people "don't wanna give" in other contexts, such as paying taxes and bills. Later on, a simple matter such as buying a holiday present for a family member can recall old feelings of, "I have to, but I hate to," or "I'll wait until the last minute to give, because I am ambivalent about this person," or "I'll give when I'm good and ready to, so don't give me deadlines." Resistance by withholding is a way to fight city hall as well as Mom.

If the child is physically ready to be trained, it's much easier and better for everyone concerned. Demands made too early can result in lifelong feelings of being overwhelmed by tasks that seem too hard. "I can't handle it," and "Forget it, it's too much for me," are common responses that come from this early experience. Problems with record keeping and learning the rules of the financial games in adulthood may also go back to this period when there was too much to cope with at one time.

Mom's response can be confusing to kids in the process of toilet training. On the one hand, she's pleased and cheers when the child "produces." This makes him want to continue to get her approval. On the other hand, she can't seem to wait to get rid of the "gift" he's given her. She flushes it down the toilet with an air of indifference which seems odd, since both Mom and child agree that the "products" are pretty important.

Later, the expression "money down the drain" will recall this earliest experience and capture the essence of the original feelings. The loss of money can feel like a personal loss, and if the loss of money is out of one's control, it can even feel humiliating or shameful. Consider how shame surfaces when mistakes are made. This feeling may be reminiscent of "accidents" in training.

Those whose training is characterized by guilt or fear of not being loved have the distinct probability of carrying around emotional scars. Later worries may take the form of attitudes such as, "I'm unworthy, undeserving, unlovable," and, "Something is wrong with me." These people discover along the way that they are treated better and appreciated more when they give money, gifts, and big tips to others. If there's excessive encouragement during toilet training, children learn that giving away valuable things gets them attention. Later, generosity compensates for their not feeling loved for themselves.

Toilet training is an extremely important influence on how people eventually use or abuse money. Such things as obedience, rebellion, submission, control, tolerance of frustration, and impulsivity are derivatives of this time of life. Later, paying bills on time, not paying taxes, taking extensions on payments, living within one's means, saving regularly, and compulsive shopping are more behaviors that come from this period.

SELF-CONTROL

Too much gratification results in self-centeredness, extreme dependency, and poor manners. That is why we teach children to control their urges as they mature. The child will learn self-control with money too. He will learn when it's inappropriate to spend money, even though he'd love to. Eventually, through experience, he'll learn he can't have everything, and he will learn to prioritize.

Just as you teach your child to have control of his bodily urges, you can teach him to have control over his spending. Self-control enables us all to plan, think, and put off gratification, and that is a worthy goal with money management. It is also what maturity is about.

With young children, you can bet on rebelliousness if your *no's* don't work and you resort to more powerful means such as spanking and other punishments. An angry child will turn his declaration of independence into a tug of war with you if you misinterpret his growing sense of uniqueness as a con to get you.

Similarly, when the child grows older and does things with money that you don't like, beware of treating the child as a rebel who needs to be quelled. Power struggles over money can touch off fireworks that include tantrums, defiance, and tears.

A pattern of no's, especially as a response to a child's request, can be very inhibiting. If your child hears *no* enough times, he'll get the picture that to be loved, he shouldn't ask for anything. He hasn't learned self-control as much as he's learned self-denial, and compulsive frugality may be the outcome. Extremely frugal people usually have feelings of insecurity and fear.

The following chapters more specifically outline methods of parenting that will encourage healthy habits and attitudes regarding money.

2

DO'S AND DON'TS FOR TEACHING THE FINANCIAL FACTS OF LIFE

THE VALUES WE TEACH KIDS ABOUT MONEY CAN ESTABLISH guidelines for a lifetime of handling their income in a confident manner. Because money can be a very complicated subject, it's worth taking a look at some pitfalls we all encounter on the road to financial maturity.

MONEY ISN'T MAGICAL

Gail was a little short of cash when it was time to pay a taxi fare. Her four-year-old daughter told her to "write out a check." She later suggested that her mother get some money "from the wall at the bank." Clearly Gail needs to explain to her daughter that money isn't magical—it can't just appear or replenish itself. Small children who see brimming supermarket baskets, bulging closets, and filled toy chests, find it hard to believe that it takes long hours at work to make it all possible.

LOVE AND MONEY AREN'T THE SAME

It's often easier to buy something for your child than to give him or her quality time, especially in this age of two-income families. When parents feel guilty for not spending time with their children, they spend money. Every airport gift shop sells novelty items to answer the inevitable question after a business trip, "What did you bring me?"

But children need to receive love, not possessions, in order to love themselves. Unfortunately, when there is more money than love available, kids believe that when their parents buy them things it means they are loved. It becomes a common misconception that the more things one has, the more love one has also.

SAYING NO CAN BE HELPFUL

Joe asked his mother for twenty dollars above his regular allowance. Mom answered with a flat no. About an hour later, Joe persisted and asked again for the extra money. This time Mom smiled and asked, "What part of *no* don't you understand?"

Saying too many no's to children's requests causes them to stop asking, but parents are not the providers of everything, and saying no helps kids to prioritize their wishes and wants. No one can have everything, but that doesn't mean we want nothing at all. Instead of saying no all the time, tell your kids what they *can* have, or teach them how to get what they want by planning ahead, establishing priorities, and shopping in a savvy way.

IT'S ALL RIGHT TO WANT THINGS

It's natural for children to be tempted by television ads and toy stores where advertisers spend lots of money to get their attention. But it's more helpful to talk about *why* your child wants certain things. For example, if your child wants what others have in order to feel like part of the gang, you need to identify what your child *really* needs. It may be a sense of security, power, or love.

Belonging, longing for leadership, popularity, and the feeling of being special are also possibilities. You can explore better ways to satisfy these needs than by buying things.

Since everybody is concerned about family finances these days, Laura thought her kids needed to understand what she meant by "a tight-money situation." When she asked if they ever heard of the words, her daughter piped up with, "It means having trouble wiggling your wallet out of tight jeans."

It's okay to *want* whatever you see. Wanting is for free. *Expecting* to have whatever you want is the problem. Let kids know what's realistic. Set limits up front so your child will know how much you have available to spend or how much you will give your child to spend on a shopping trip, and stick to that amount.

WHAT MONEY IS FOR

Money is a means to an end, not the end itself. It's not worth going to jail for, nor is it worth the risk of losing one's integrity or reputation.

Money is the means for taking care of yourself by paying bills, preparing for a secure future, and buying things to make life more pleasant. Money is for charitable gifts to strangers and for general gift-giving among friends and relations. It's for serious investing and for having fun, too.

ENVY AND JEALOUSY

We all feel twitches of envy from time to time, but constantly wishing that we had what seems to bring pleasure to others can also produce resentment and outright hostility. Criticism becomes a device that tears down the envied object to make it seem less desirable. Kids need to know that possessions do not equal worthiness. Help kids enjoy their belongings and share what they have so they'll learn about the pride of ownership and social responsibility.

MANIPULATION WITH MONEY

Once children learn that money is a powerful substance, they may abuse it. They may borrow money from friends and forget to pay it back. They may loan money to make a friend. Offering bribes and doing favors for money are some ways kids wheel and deal.

But children need to be taught there are more appropriate ways to feel powerful, such as by being a leader, speaking up in assertive ways, and taking responsibility.

MONEY IS FOR FUN AS WELL AS NECESSITIES

One mother asked her child what he learned in school that day. The child answered, "Mixed greens are good for you, especially fives, tens, and twenties."

While you don't want to encourage your child to throw money around or minimize its importance, it's part of life to have fun with money. When you give them a little extra money now and then, kids can indulge themselves with an occasional impulse purchase, a treat, or a souvenir without feeling guilty.

By treating yourself to a spontaneous purchase, you can show your child that money is not *just* for necessities.

TEACH HOW TO PLAN, PRIORITIZE, SAVE, AND SHOP

Young children don't have much conception about time, as this story illustrates. Uncle Charles gave his nephew a cash gift for his birthday, and then they took a forty-mile automobile trip to the big city to spend it. Every few miles, Mike asked his uncle, "Are we there yet?" After hearing this question over and over, Uncle Charles impatiently told him, "It will be a long time yet." Mike then asked, "Will my twenty-dollar bill still be worth twenty when we get there?"

Helping children learn to plan ahead, save, and prioritize involves time and patience, but these lessons are the most valuable financial facts of life they can learn.

ALLOW YOUR CHILD TO MAKE MISTAKES

It wasn't long after Carolyn and her mother decided on a weekly amount of money for her that she complained, "There are too many days left at the end of my allowance." That anxious feeling is the best teacher, because it's so uncomfortable that most of us will do something to avoid it.

When kids do not get advances, they will budget better, figure out how to earn some extra money for what they want, or do without. Those who get extra money only learn to ask for more.

Now that you know the fundamental do's and don'ts of teaching children about money, let's take a look at how these lessons can be applied to each age group.

Part Two

Age-Appropriate Money Lessons

3

YOUR SIX
TO SEVEN
YEAR OLD

As THE BELL RANG, JENNIE JUMPED UP FROM THE SOFA AND RAN to open the door. "Grandma's here!" she yelled. "Where's my present?" "That's a fine howdy-do," said Grandma, stunned by the question.

Was Jennie's question so surprising? After all, Grandma had come to visit many times laden with gifts of all variations. She always had some sourball candy and chewing gum in her purse, as well as a few novelty items to delight and distract Jennie when the visit needed some excitement. In Grandma's time it was impolite to say what one thought. Now, kids expect and even demand gifts, since they frequently receive many.

While we all want direct, honest, and assertive children, you must let them know when their behavior goes beyond what you consider reasonable. You might say, "It's great to have Grandma here and that's the most important thing." It's not necessary to embarrass the child on the spot with words such as, "Jennie, what kind of thing is that for you to say?" Nor is it the time to hide your own face in horror over her poor manners. Later, at a quiet time, you can let your child know that you are aware of what she felt and that it was understandable that she said what she did. Then tell her the effect her question had on Grandma and you. Empathizing with her feelings opens the discussion in a noncritical way. Stick to the facts of what happened: Jennie was excited. Grandma was startled. Ask for some thoughts on why they each felt the way they did. Then come up with a better way to greet Grandma in the future, such as, "Hi, Grandma. I'm so glad to see you. I can't wait to play with you!" No doubt, Grandma will carry the ball from there.

THE JOY OF POSSESSIONS

What seems to be a grabby, materialistic attitude on Jennie's part is fairly typical of most six year olds. Sixes have both the expectation and the hope of receiving something, because collecting is a big part of this age. Quantity is important to the six year old, even if she doesn't necessarily play with all her possessions. She can be rather careless about her belongings, in fact, and sometimes treats them badly. *Having* the possessions seems to be more important than holding onto them, though, since losing or misplacing things is also common.

Some six year olds, on the other hand, delight in giving away their toys and can be generous to a fault. This child is maturing and discovering new personal powers. She can make choices and decisions. Since this is often a stressful or bewildering experience, there are occasional shifts from one behavior to the other.

The next time you give your child some change to buy something in a novelty store, you'll see how difficult it can be for her to make a decision. She may meander around for a very long time before making a choice. Then, after taking inventory of the store, she may choose something that is totally irrelevant to her interests but costs the right amount of money. A friend of mine has a vivid memory of buying lavender Sen-Sen, the Tic Tac of forty years ago, not because she enjoyed the taste, but because she had the right number of pennies to pay for it.

WANTS VERSUS NEEDS

Making an observation such as, "I see you had a hard time finding something you wanted," can open a conversation that can lead to a discussion about *wants* as opposed to *needs*. She *wanted* to have a fancy pencil, for example, even though her pencil box had a few in it already. She *needed* a new notebook, since hers was almost out of paper. Your discussion can move toward more serious subjects too, such as the difference between having to take drugs to cure illness and experimenting with drugs.

Wish or desire compared to necessity may seem like a fine line to draw with children. Try making a list of the necessities of life and then embellishing them with customized accoutrements to get the point across. For example, children can understand the need for a house to live in, while the style of it may be something merely wanted, such as a log cabin, a tent, or a penthouse in the sky. We need food for survival, but how we cook it or whether we go to a restaurant for it has to do with what we want. Everybody needs clothing, but what store we go to and what style we pick has to do with buying what we want. Our needs *have* to be met, but our wants can't always be satisfied.

My son, Eric, wanted a skateboard so badly he sounded like he needed one. He saw some big boys having fun while sliding around on them. They made it look so easy to zig and zag as they barreled down the hilly sidewalk. I wasn't so happy to hear his plaintive cries for a toy that seemed to demand more coordination than a six year old could muster. I envisioned bruised knees and worse. However, I came up with a compromise. He wanted to buy the toy, and I wanted to buy some time, so I told him that he could have a skateboard as long as he helped to pay for it. [Since he was getting an allowance already, I suggested that I add some money to this allowance that could be earmarked for it.] He agreed, and we negotiated a reasonable amount that he would have to save before getting the skateboard. I think we arrived at three dollars. It took nearly a year until he saved that amount in the clear plastic bank on his desk. He barely brought up the subject during that time, and for that I was truly grateful. I thought, or I hoped, he'd forget about it and set his sights on something less dangerous, but he didn't. As promised, we made a trip to the big toy store with the grandest selection of skateboards, and, fortunately, he chose a relatively cheap red one. He loved it even though he never mastered it. *Having* it was the most important thing to him. Teaching him to save was important to me, and subsequently he went on to save for other toys he wanted.

THE GIMMES

Kids, by age six, watch television, see commercials, and want the products they see. If "The Gimmes" don't get you at the store, they'll surely get you on Saturday mornings after the kiddy shows. Since children don't have a real conception of cost yet, there seems to be no limit to their requests.

Setting limits, however, is an extremely important parental duty which kids must experience and parents sometimes dread. There are parents who want to be "nice guys" and who have trouble saying no, but it is in the child's best interest to have limits imposed. No one can have everything, even parents with checkbooks and credit cards, and kids have to learn this.

Marsha came up with a very clever idea to tame the temptations of TV. Rather than saying no to her son every time he asked her to buy something, she told him to make a picture of what he wanted and put it into a big envelope. She made it clear to him that he could have what he wanted from that portfolio for his birthday and at holiday time only. Periodically, they would review the pictures and add new ones or toss out some that had lost their initial interest. When occasions arose where relatives wanted to know "what Todd wanted these days," Marsha had a ready supply of his wish-list items to suggest. As a result, Todd managed to get some of what he wanted while he learned the value of having patience.

THE ALLOWANCE

The allowance is the best tool for teaching kids the financial facts of life. Not only does it offer the opportunity to work on some pretty good life skills, such as negotiating, being responsible, and setting priorities, but it is a tool for learning money management. It teaches budgeting, saving, and how to make spending decisions.

When a child is six or seven and in school, there may be a need to carry some money for lunches, snacks, and transportation. Introducing an allowance is important at this time. Consider the types of expenses the child has, how much he needs for discretionary spending, when the money will be given, what can happen if extra needs come up, what to do with money left over at the end of the week, and a bit about your recognition that the child is grown up enough to be "allowed" an allowance.

Of course, they will initially spend the money too fast and will have to do without before the end of the month is up. The feeling can be so uncomfortable that it will be avoided forever after—and that's the point. Limits are a part of life, and spending within limits is our goal, but children will not reach that goal until they've made mistakes. Perhaps you'll be courageous enough to share some of your spending experiences with your kids as they goof along the way. Their mistakes will help them learn to make decisions about financial priorities.

When they run short of money, don't give them any advances, or you'll defeat the whole purpose of limiting them with an allowance. They'll get the idea that they will be bailed out like Chrysler and the Savings and Loans if they get into trouble. They'll think twice, or at least a little ahead, next time. "Next time" has a soft and forgiving ring to it, by the way. I recommend that phrase for all sorts of situations.

One issue to be avoided is the allowance mentality; that of being "on the dole." We are not giving a handout to the child; nor is the child to be put into a position of asking for money with a hand out like a beggar. Negotiating the amount of the allowance ought to include a little extra for whatever the child wants over the established needs. If only necessities are covered, the lessons about money are incomplete. Remember, money is for fun as well as for fixed needs. When I give talks to parents' groups, I ask, "How many of you were told to have fun with money?" Generally, there are only a few hands that go up.

There are some parents who insist that their children are too young for the responsibility of having an allowance. They want the kids to come to them for money and don't mind being asked. It may seem generous at first, but the child is put into a position of having to defend his desire for the purchase under consideration and may feel like a beggar in the process. The parent becomes a judge in deciding whether the request is valid. Over time, the child may simply limit requests, to avoid the discomfort of asking, and he certainly will not have the opportunity to learn money-management skills.

Often, parents see the allowance as a means to control children. Resentment comes as a result of power struggles, which the child usually cannot win and from which he can only gain bad feelings. He will also lose self-esteem and motivation. An allowance with no strings attached produces a sense of security and independence, and since the six-year-old child will probably be saving most of his spare change, he will be learning a good lesson also.

ALLOWANCE TIPS

When parents ask me for pointers on the allowance, I try to convey the idea that the parent allows the child to have something worthwhile—money—because learning to use it, not abuse it, is very important. Money is merely a means of exchange. Yet, the complexity of emotions attached to money accounts for what money may *symbolize* but cannot buy, such as security, power, love, and independence.

A six-year-old child does not know the worth of what he buys. He can barely understand the difference between a nickel and a dime. He'll often prefer a nickel since it's bigger and seems more valuable. He'll probably prefer two nickels to a dime since quantity seems a better deal. By the slow process of experiencing what the coins can get him in return, he'll eventually learn value, but he has to have money for this to take place.

Determine a specific amount of the allowance. Unless there are special financial needs upon which you and the child agree, start the allowance with a couple of dollars and add a dollar at each birthday.

Your awareness of the expenses you usually incur for your child's snacks can be a good start, as well as the amount your child's friends receive. Too small an allowance will be inhibiting, since the child will feel hopeless if he's too poor to purchase anything; too much money, on the other hand, can be overwhelming.

Determine exactly what expenses are to come from the allowance. Your child will learn the worth of the coins as he buys things such as soda, gum, or fruit. If you don't want the child to buy candy bars, for example, that can be discussed at the outset when you are figuring out the specifics of the allowance. Talk about the different kinds of snacks that would be more nutritious. However, be aware that kids use their discretionary money to buy things you probably frown on, and candy bars fit that category.

Let the child know what expenses he is to take care of and what he can continue to count on you to handle. This eliminates a lot of hassles.

When infractions of the rules occur, you can always refer back to your initial conversation when the rules were made. Putting the rules in writing will also eliminate quarrels.

It is usually best for the parent to give the allowance on Sunday, since that is the beginning of the week and the child can start out with a jingle in his pocket. Sundays are usually more relaxed, so the possibility of forgetting to give the money is decreased. It is important to make a set time to give it, perhaps before bedtime, and not to wait to be asked for it. You would not like to have to ask for your salary, would you? You would not like to have to hang around until your boss arbitrarily decided to pay you.

Similarly, you would not appreciate it if your boss told you what to buy or when to spend your money. Nor would you be particularly happy if your boss docked your pay if you or your work did not please him. For these reasons, it does not make sense to criticize or punish with the allowance. There are other ways to monitor behavior.

Give your child a colorful change purse or wallet to celebrate the special occasion of starting an allowance. This might help to keep the coins out of the washing machine at the same time that it acts as a reminder that money is important enough to be kept in a special place. If your child doesn't have a box or a small bank, look around the kitchen for some kind of container, such as a cup, yogurt container, or an unbreakable glass. A bank is a perfect birthday present for this age group. It's also a great rainy-day project to make one. Since cigar boxes are not so readily available, an oatmeal box, or a small box such as individual portions of juice come in, would work. Your child can decorate it with colored paper, stickers, and other creative materials.

Kids like to see how much money they have, and they like to be able to count it, so a bank, such as a jelly jar, that offers those benefits would be best. The old-fashioned piggy banks gobbled up the coins and had to be broken open to get at the contents. They were piggys, indeed, for keeping the coins out of circulation. Perhaps there's a place for forced savings, but watching pennies pile up can encourage saving also.

My son used an empty gin bottle as a place to store pennies. It got so heavy, it could barely be lifted. I'm embarrassed to say that this bottle has stood on a living-room table for years. It is a fixture which our family has come to appreciate, since we all add to it when our own pennies become too numerous to lug around.

CHORES FOR CASH

Some parents lament that their kids seem to be irresponsible not only with money but also in helping out with chores in the home. Actually, there is a link between money and chores in both negative and positive ways. When the allowance gets cut because the child didn't set the table, the child learns to feel resentment and sees that the allowance is not something he can count on. If he gets his allowance only when he's good, he'll surely associate money with love and eventually may confuse the two. Children need to know that their allowance will be theirs whether they're good or not. Remember, you are allowing your child to have that money—that's why it's called an *allowance*.

If the child is told that the allowance is part of the family's money, and he gets it because he is part of the family, he'll be more willing to pitch in with chores for the same reason. It feels more constructive and, of course, we all respond better to rewards than to punishments.

Show your appreciation and keep criticism to a minimum. Even if the dishes are put into the dishwasher backwards, they'll get clean. Sooner or later they'll be facing the right direction, if kids don't experience you as commanding them. If you're pleased to have their help and the expectations aren't too high, they'll probably help more.

Kids who want extra money can earn it by doing odd jobs around the house. If there is a bonus for doing more than the expected, the child has motivation to do it. Make a Chore Chart of possible things to do and what you'd be willing to pay for having them done. Then involve your child by asking what chores he might add to the list. He can even draw pictures of the jobs on the chart or write in the money amount.

Chores such as unpacking grocery bags, starting and emptying the dishwasher, and watering plants can be made more agreeable with bonuses. Use stars or stickers to show how much each chore is worth. The tougher the job, the more stars it deserves. Not only will the child have a good feeling from negotiating this with you, but she will begin to sense the value of participating in home life and see her role in it. That may be more important than the actual coins earned for spending or saving. After all, no one can put a monetary value on the glint in a mother's eye, which signifies the parental seal of approval. That look is what *really* motivates. Kids want to please, so let them know what pleases.

PRACTICAL AND FUN THINGS TO DO

Kids know their numbers by age six. They can count by ones to thirty or so and by tens to a hundred. They can add numbers up to ten, usually, and by age seven will name the coins and tell you how many pennies there are in a nickel or a dime. Playing with coins can be fun as long as it feels like a game and not a lesson.

A deck of playing cards is useful at this age, since kids like them and they lend themselves to money games easily. Perhaps you can improvise your own counting games with cards.

Kids learn best when they are active participants. Since they are not always eager to learn arithmetic in any formal way, life experiences are meaningful and much more interesting.

Shopping excursions are wonderful opportunities for kids to make practical use of their knowledge about coins and numbers. When you get change, give it to your child to count. When you leave a tip if you stop for a snack, tell your child how much you want to give and see if your child can help count out the change. When you stop for a soda or ice-cream cone, hand the money to your child to give to the clerk, and if there's change, have the child count it. Perhaps you'll let him keep it for buying something later.

You might also borrow this classroom exercise. After a field trip, a teacher usually discusses the experience with the class to help the children remember the fine points. Then the class expresses their trip experience through artwork, drama, songs, and so forth. You can do this too by recalling some of the things done with money on the shopping trip, then making a project to reflect those things. Since kids this age like to color, drawing a picture would be one possibility. To build your child's self-esteem, hang the picture or display the project for everyone to admire.

GOALS OF AGE SIX TO SEVEN

• Differentiate between wants and needs.

• Make a "wish list" and then prioritize it.

• Start an allowance.

• Experience spending.

• Make some mistakes to learn some limits of the allowance.

• Establish possibilities for earning bonuses.

• Begin saving in a bank at home.

• Learn the values of coins.

• Use life experiences as lessons in handling money.

4

YOUR SEVEN
TO EIGHT
YEAR OLD

LIVING WITHIN ONE'S MEANS

TALKING ABOUT LIVING WITHIN ONE'S MEANS DOESN'T HAVE to be a lecture. The first time your child runs out of money or wants something that costs too much, gently let her know that this is a common problem which everybody, including you, experiences from time to time. Analyze her spending habits to determine what she spent her money on that caused her to run short. This will help you find out if the amount of money you've allotted for extras is realistic. Then ask your child for some ideas on how she might plan better next week. Remind her that if she saves a little of her allowance each week, the amount can add up sufficiently so that she can borrow from herself when she runs short. If she wants to do something extra to earn some money, refer to your Chore Chart.

To convey the value of money to your child, you must not make it readily accessible to her. Instead, encourage saving and planning. Eventually, the child will learn to think about whether she can afford the second piece of pizza. She will figure out how many days remain before her coffers get refilled and whether she can tolerate being broke if she spends her allowance too early in the week. The feeling of not having money is a painful, potent signal. If children don't get to experience it, they won't learn to manage their money as well. The seven year old is ready for this money-management lesson.

An excellent tool for teaching kids about careful spending, especially if they are having difficulty budgeting, is a daily diary. If your child lists everything she spent money on for a week, there will be no mystery about where the money went. Small purchases do add up, as we all know, and the diary is useful in showing the child on what types of things she's spending the most money.

The diary can also be useful if your child wants to save money for something special. By consulting her list, she can determine where she can cut back on expenditures. You can brainstorm with your child on this, but always ask her for ideas first. She might come up with a strategy where she'll do without everything for a while. If you think she's being too severe with herself, let her know there are options that are less harsh. Perhaps she'd like to take snacks from home rather than buying them, or maybe she'll spend less by buying an apple instead of a piece of pizza. If she likes the snack-from-home idea, ask her what she'd like you to purchase on your trip to the supermarket. This will show her that you are willing to cooperate while she is learning to budget; however, if snacks from the corner store are important, ask her what she'd be willing to temporarily give up for a while until she has the money she needs. Could it be walking instead of taking a bus? Playing fewer video games? Skipping a movie or cutting back on baseball cards? With a limited amount of money to spend, your child will learn to prioritize, cut back, cut out, or try to earn more through doing bonus chores or by coming up with a money-making idea of her own. If you merely bail your child out of her financial difficulties early on, she will surely believe that money is available merely for the asking.

The daily diary can also show at what times spending occurs. The circumstances surrounding purchases, time of day, day of the week, and so on may be very important, especially if there is an obvious pattern. For example, let's say your child buys himself excessive treats after school on the days he has his least-favorite subject or has a class with a teacher he doesn't particularly like. Using treats to reward yourself for getting through a difficult experience is not appropriate. Life is full of tough days. By connecting the treat to his emotions, you can help your child talk about finding better ways to cope instead of automatically reacting to problems with treats.

CHILDREN AS CONSUMERS

Since children spend billions of dollars a year, advertisers strive for product loyalty, especially when there is a good chance that the brand preferences at age seven will be the same at seventeen. Advertisers spend huge amounts on advertisements. There are about twenty-four commercials per hour during the Saturday-morning kids' shows. No wonder kids want their parents to buy them things. It's easy to see how kids become materialistic too. Parents can limit the amount of time for TV and tone down the effects of television ads by talking about them.

James U. McNeal, Ph.D., marketing professor at Texas A. & M., studies children's buying habits from age four to age twelve. He found that children are a perfect target audience, since they recognize products from commercials, get parents to purchase them, and remain loyal to brand names for many years. Children spend billions of dollars a year of their own for food, clothing, and fun. Most of this discretionary income comes from paid chores, gifts from relatives, and part-time jobs. McNeal estimates that children save about twenty percent of what they get overall, and that's a tidy sum too, which explains why many banks are interested in your children's money as well.

Let's look at the influence of advertising on children who are only seven or eight. Advertisers know that kids will want what their friends have, so first they spend a lot of money to get their merchandise noticed. Then they hope enough kids will buy the merchandise and stimulate others to buy. Since making advertisements and putting them on television or in the newspaper is expensive, kids ought to know that the cost of advertising gets passed along to them when they buy things. Just because the ad is big or appears often doesn't make the product good, just more expensive.

Because prices are not generally included in the commercials, it often appears to young children that toys are free. If the price is mentioned, it may be in the context of "It's *only* $14.95," which implies that it's a real bargain and parents can't argue that it costs too much. This advertising ploy should also be brought to your child's attention.

The seven to eight year old begins to be influenced by peer pressure when making consumer choices. Before your child decides on a purchase, talk about what it is your child says he wants or needs and see if there is a follow-the-leader aspect involved which can be discussed further. Sometimes there are underlying issues of self-esteem, peer pressure, or other issues that your child hopes to salve, if not solve, with money. While fitting in with his friends is important to a child, you must again stress that no one can have everything and that if the desired item is so important, saving is one way to obtain it.

ADVERTISING PROMISES

Advertisements promise such things as popularity, athletic prowess, and good looks. Kids need to know that these promises are impossible to deliver. The blue jeans can't reshape your body and the sneakers can't turn you into an athletic wonder. Advertisers try to make their products seem like the answer to childhood dilemmas. In an age of Band-Aids, cough drops, and other quick fixes, children get the idea that "things" can make them feel better. Similarly, children like to feel older and stronger. G.I. Joe paraphernalia, swords, and guns make kids feel that they are powerful. Toys for grown-ups do the same. High-tech items, leather goods, and luxury fabrics are shorthand symbols of prestige and power. Guns make adults feel more secure also.

Children are pleased when they recognize something that is advertised on television. Songs and advertising jingles are easy to remember, and their repetition usually make parents laugh. But when advertising promises are not met, children suffer the consequences.

Alexandra remembers saving cereal box tops for a pedometer, a device to strap to her ankle that could tell how many miles she walked. The picture on the cereal box led Alexandra to believe that she'd love this shiny, sturdy toy and that her friends would admire and respect her for having it. The pedometer was touted as being "Olympic quality" and an "official timepiece." It took months to get enough box tops, then more time until it finally arrived. The pedometer looked like a big wristwatch, weighed only a couple of ounces, and rattled when she shook it. After trying it out, Alexandra realized the meter didn't move, so she threw it away, having learned a difficult lesson about the promises inherent in advertising.

PREMIUMS AND PACKAGING

Kids are vulnerable to packaging ploys as well. Young children want the prize enclosed rather than the contents of the box, especially if their friends have whatever premium is inside. The cereal, however, may linger on the pantry shelf longer than your child's interest in the toy. Parents pressured into buying a product once won't fall for it a second time if stuck with uneaten food.

Kids ought to know that nothing is totally free, even though it appears the manufacturer of the product is giving a toy away. Kids at age seven can understand that advertisers want them to buy their brand of cereal, and so the extra toy is inside to help sell more, but for a family there is no benefit to uneaten food. If your child insists on trying new products repeatedly, simply for the pleasure of owning the premium, suggest he buy the cereal with his allowance money.

As for the words, nutrition information, and pictures on the packages, reading as many of them as she can is a good exercise for a child. Does the cereal contain fresh strawberries because they're featured in the bowl on the front? Do the nutrients listed supply essential vitamins and minerals? Does the word "natural" appear on the packaging but a preservative appear on the ingredients list? These are all ways to teach children of this age group to understand marketing tools. On a trip to the supermarket, see if your child will help you buy something salt-free, low in sugar, or "lite," and talk about what that means. Begin comparison shopping for quality as well as price.

You might show your child a newly opened box of cereal and comment about how big the box is but that it's only filled three-quarter full. You can explain that the contents weigh what the number says on the box and that the food settles a bit while it sits on the shelf. Nevertheless, the manufacturers want you to think you're getting more because the box is big.

NAME BRANDS

The use of brand names is noticeable to kids by age seven. Just ask a child to draw a picture of a soda and you will see the name of his favorite drink right there on its label. Toys such as trucks, toy gas stations, and play housewares display name-brand decals for realism. This is not by accident. Names are important to kids, especially their own, so brand names are a natural way to distinguish a product.

Name brands do cost more because of the expense involved in making them familiar through advertising. We often justify the additional expense by saying that they are made better, look smarter, and last longer. We feel trust in products that have been around a long time. This is what we call quality, and many people are willing to use their hard-earned dollars to get it.

Kids want to conform and are under considerable pressure to do so from their peers. Since there are too many choices out there, brand names help kids make the "right choice." They feel validated when others have similar things. Again, it is important for children to determine quality and not just be pressured to buy a name.

LEARNING ABOUT HYPE

Some advertisers make promises and even threats of regret if you don't buy their merchandise, so it's possible to feel confused and fall for a hyped-up product rather than for one that is perfectly okay, but without the fancy ads. It's fun to take a look at some ads in the newspaper or to look at the cleaning supplies in the closet to see what is labeled the newest, the most improved, and the most miraculous. To desensitize children to TV commercials, try making a game of repeating the claims as they watch the advertisements. See who can repeat the commercial fastest or loudest. By making children aware of the promises being made, you will allow them to catch on to the sales techniques rather than be caught up in them.

On a rainy day, instead of a story, try to make a game of finding the facts about different products. Ask your child what the product is supposed to accomplish. This will show if your child gets the point of an ad. Kids who are too young to read the ads can listen to you and tell you what facts are memorable. They can look at the pictures in magazine ads and tell you a story about what they see. Ask your child to figure out what the big deal is if a lot of dentists recommend a certain brand of toothpaste or if more doctors give Brand X to their patients. Even though they love magic at this age, do they really think that it's possible for clothes to get whiter than white? Or for people, animals, or talking fruit to suddenly appear in your home? Question other promises, such as whether products can make people younger, healthier, and more important. Explain that commercials have camera tricks which are just that—tricks to make a product more appealing or memorable.

Ads can show children, women, and older people in odd ways. It can be fun to ask kids what they make of the women who are disgusted by soap scum on the bathroom wall or the children who mindlessly eat one candy bar after another. Sometimes relationships in ads are worth talking about, since some families don't have puttering grandfathers or working dads. Talking about working-mom ads can give a big clue to your child's attitude toward you, if you work. It's also an opportunity to talk about the beautiful people in ads who are more fantasy figures than real people.

GOALS OF AGE SEVEN TO EIGHT

- **Begin to save and plan for future spending.**

- **Make a daily diary for expenditures.**

- **Prioritize expenses and explore cutting some cost.**

- **Discuss the promises of advertisements.**

- **Learn about packaging, premiums, and hype.**

YOUR EIGHT TO NINE YEAR OLD

THE LEMONADE STAND

WILLIAM WAS NO LONGER INTERESTED IN HIS SESAME STREET toys and wanted a computer game, so he decided to see if he could have a "yard sale" near the bus stop on Madison Avenue. He invited his buddy, Josh, to stand with him while he tried to sell books, toys, and Kool Aid. William put prices on stick-on labels, and shopped at the supermarket for just the right size paper cups for the Kool Aid, and put a great deal of effort into organizing his stand. He sold some toys and books and then promptly divided his profits with his best friend. But as soon as William brought home the remaining inventory, he and Josh were out again to buy comic books at the newsstand. They were much better at shopping than managing their entrepreneurial ventures. The idea of profit and saving was suddenly elusive, but money in the pocket was understandable.

Eight is the age of the lemonade stand. Variations on this theme could be any entrepreneurial endeavor from selling grapefruits on a dirt road in Tucson with very few potential customers to a corner stand on Madison Avenue in New York City. Money is the major motivating factor, and for the eight year old, a lot of money could be five dollars.

The lemonade stand, or its equivalent, comes about at this time because kids watch adults work and want to mimic them. They like to appear to be grown up, and certainly being in a "business" helps. They want the financial rewards too, since they appreciate the fact that the more money they have, the more it becomes possible to have the things they desire.

By this age, kids know the value of coins and they can add and subtract and make change. As a result, their involvement with money takes on new meaning for them.

There are many lessons to be learned from the lemonade stand or its variations. The process of pulling together the supplies, making the drinks or cookies, setting up the merchandise, labeling or pricing items helps to organize the child and to let him experience the many small parts that go into the whole endeavor. The child needs patience to wait for customers and to wait on them. Relating to strangers' questions and taking care of transactions is not easy. These kids haven't taken courses in selling techniques. They're copying what they've observed from adults' sales behavior.

If there are other children involved, then there's a good chance that what starts as a cooperative venture can erupt in fights over how to manage the business. Solving these problems is also a learning experience.

Kids gain self-confidence by going through the motions of being in business. They see that they can handle the job they set out to accomplish. Their used toys and books get a new home, and they have new space to fill in their own home. The biggest benefit is that they get money for their efforts.

As for the business lessons, children learn about profit, overhead, inventory, net profit, and making change, even if they're unfamiliar with these terms. Profits may not cover the expense of the cups and liquid refreshments they sell, and that may come as a real surprise to the children. By keeping whatever receipts they got when they bought supplies, and subtracting this amount from their profit, they will learn what *net profit* means. They may also discover that *overhead*, the cost of being in business, is expensive.

SELF-ESTEEM AND MONEY

The pleasures of cash flow become apparent to eight year olds. Conversely, they may feel that without money they are losers in general. Children need to learn that having money is certainly nice, but it does not define who they are or whether they are okay. Self-esteem has to be built on overcoming challenges and taking risks, not from the roll of some dice if they are playing a game.

Unfortunately, even grownups have some confusion between net worth and self-worth. "What's he worth?" may be a common question children hear during dinner conversations. Too many people pin their self-worth to their assets and bottom lines. There was even a study done on stockbrokers' libidos and the Dow Jones industrial average. When the Dow was up and the bull market was raging, their libido was up, and when the crash came tumbling down, so did their sex life.

Kids can learn to protect their self-esteem from erosive factors such as comparing themselves to others. Thinking less of themselves if they cannot afford the toys others have, or deferring to others because they are richer, are destructive behaviors. The eight to nine year old is ready to learn to accept himself and others for who they are, not what they own.

Discussions about how money makes people feel and act can be natural occurrences after playing Monopoly or seeing a show on television that includes this theme. If your child follows the sports news, there's plenty of opportunity to talk about the gigantic salaries the sports figures get for their performance, not for whether they are nice people. Some occupations pay a lot of money, while others with great social value don't pay as well. Kids need to know that rock stars with millions of dollars don't necessarily feel better about themselves than teachers or hospital workers, who earn a lot less. Ask them what they think about a society that values entertainers so much and voice your opinion, too.

Your child can build self-esteem by doing things and then patting himself on the back. At this age, kids don't like to be told what to do, so ask what their idea of helping around the house might be. Fixing or improving something, making a special dish for dinner, or transplanting a plant might be self-esteem boosters.

Taking a bus ride alone or buying the newspaper for you and counting the change feels very grown up and good too.

COLLECTING

Eight year olds also love collecting. My son, Eric, got the comic-book bug, and his closet was never used for clothing again. He removed the hardware and made a wooden bookshelf that fit inside the closet to hold the long, "professional-size" cardboard boxes of his favorites. Over the years, he organized the comics, made an inventory list, and bagged them lovingly in plastic, acid-free containers. They're still there, even though he's in medical school. I've had my eye on that closet for years, but there's no indication yet that the collection is ripe for sale.

Eric gained a lot of respect when he was an "X-Man" expert at the Big Apple comics store. When I told him that I could no longer support his collecting habit, he was quick to find a solution by getting a part-time job where he could get paid with comics. His job was to sit on a high stool and field questions from his peers. He conveyed enough enthusiasm to generate considerable sales and his self-esteem grew from the respect he felt from the customers.

Collecting is a big deal for children. They get a lot of ego gratification from showing off the quantity and quality of their collections. They spend a lot of time and energy caring for their possessions, and they feel a challenge in filling in the holes in whatever it is they collect. Some kids use a baseball-card collection as the basis for play dates, and some, such as Eric, seek an identity through their collection. He wanted to be known as the kid with the biggest collection of comics.

Children without siblings might turn to their collection for amusement and to stave off loneliness. Active involvement with the collection beats sitting around passively watching television, too. Collections help all kids to occupy their time and offer a great deal of gratification, especially if parents aren't available to spend time with them. For more information on collectibles, see chapter 9.

BARTERING

Bartering can also build self-esteem. If starting a lemonade stand doesn't suit your child, possessions that she's outgrown can be traded for somebody else's. Perhaps she could keep a Barter Box in the closet that could be dipped into for trading purposes. This could be a way to build something like a dollhouse collection while preparing to give away former treasures that have lost their luster.

In some cases, kids want only brand-new toys, even if they don't play with them very much. It seems that used toys are not valued, and this needs to be turned around. When kids trade toys instead of inheriting them as hand-me-downs, they learn that all things have worth, and they won't feel so envious of their older sibling who seems to get everything new.

Since having and holding onto things are hallmarks of this age group, there is probably some underlying anxiety involved. A good talk could unearth some clues about what is truly important to your child. Competitiveness, the search for being unique, or the fear of not having enough might be the real issues.

Kids see how you handle clutter. If you are a pack rat, then you might think about doing a barter deal too. What might you look for in exchange for your rarely used treasures? A couple of hours of baby-sitting? A room painted? Some other household service? It's possible that some of the things in the garage or basement that are still good could be someone else's payment for chores or services you don't want to do yourself.

GOALS OF AGE EIGHT TO NINE

- **Become aware of how money is a part of daily living.**

- **Make change.**

- **Understand concepts such as profit, overhead, inventory, and net profit.**

- **Enjoy collecting and organizing things.**

- **Try bartering.**

- **Separate having money and feeling good from being a good person.**

- **Do things to build self-esteem that don't involve money.**

6

YOUR NINE TO TEN YEAR OLD

A TEACHER ASKED HER CLASS, "WHO KNOWS WHAT A BANK vault looks like?" Samantha's hand shot up and she said, "It's a big dark place in the basement where piggy banks with everybody's names on them are kept."

Indeed, there are lots of misperceptions about banks and money, but by this age kids can get their ideas straightened out and even open their own accounts with your help. Kids at this age want to know about money and how things like banks work.

SAVINGS ACCOUNTS

At this age, kids are in that middle zone between being a child and an adolescent. They could be called "tweens." They still need to be reminded to do things, yet they are also self-motivated and will accomplish whatever they put their mind to do. Since their attention span is longer, they will work at things repeatedly until they get them right. This persistence usually helps kids feel mastery and a sense of self-esteem. Their businesslike behavior for making inventories of their collections is a sign of their maturing organizational abilities. Unfortunately, they may be disorganized about their allowance. Because they want to please, they are even more apt to do things to help out without asking for money. Yet, they do have a growing sense of fairness and don't want to be cheated or taken advantage of. In fact, they do have a critical ability to size up friends and family as well as themselves and can spot wrongdoing pretty easily. Their conscience is developing and they can understand lying, cheating, and stealing. Since they are able to plan ahead and can follow through on tasks, once they know the steps, this is a good age to focus on a saving program. Kids this age can make regular trips to the bank and can appreciate the record keeping involved. They're good at facts and figures, so keeping track of savings with a passbook can be a source of pleasure.

It seems that there are two types of people: those who save and those who wish they could; yet almost everyone agrees that saving is a good idea. Even if you don't save money, you can show your child the basics of how to do it. While it may be more difficult, teaching your child may be an opportunity for you to learn this good habit together.

On the other hand, you might be saving money, but your kids don't see you do it. If you deposit your paycheck in the bank on your way home from work, or bank by mail or by computer, your children won't experience you as a saver, and it will be more difficult for them to get into the habit themselves. Saving is a difficult thing to do, since the pressures to spend and to have things right away are strong. The concept of saving means delaying gratification until the distant future. Unless there is a concrete goal to use as motivation to save, it won't happen. Until about this age, kids don't think of the future much beyond next summer or the next birthday. The challenge is to introduce saving in a way that emphasizes its positives rather than the negatives. You can't force a child to save, but you can convey the benefits of doing so.

Other ideas to explore with your child are the reasons to save money in the bank. If your child gets money gifts from you or his grandparents that are too big to keep at home safely, that is a reason to open an account.

Think of opening an account so your child won't be tempted to spend everything he has saved. Once he's got a goal, such as wanting a camera or a bicycle, that is the best reason to put money away. A goal makes saving more real. Have him place a picture of what he wants on the bureau in his room. If there's enough money saved, interest can help him reach the goal a little faster. Long-range goals such as a car or a college education can be coupled with a short-range goal to make saving more fun.

Kids don't have too much money until they start to work, so you might consider the idea of matching funds, to make it less of a strain to reach a reasonable goal. Matching the amount of money your child saves is great motivation and will encourage saving in even the most resistant children.

With all the emphasis on security these days, it makes good sense to take care of money by protecting it from fire and theft too. Saving for opportunities or emergencies are more reasons to put money aside in the bank.

It's also a good idea to tell kids what *you* are saving for, so they can understand that they also must set a goal and plan how to meet it. If you "pay yourself first," as financial planners advise, then your kids will probably do so too. When you give your child an allowance, suggest that some of it, maybe ten percent, be put back into a bank at home right away rather than taking the chance that some money will be left over at the end of the week. Children begin to value saving more when they put the money away first, rather than only saving the leftovers from their allowance.

KIDS' CONCERNS ABOUT BANKS

When you talk to your child about saving money in a bank, there are some concerns to keep in mind. Kids have funny ideas of what happens to their money once they hand it over to the teller. Some worry that they'll never see it again because it will get mixed up with everybody else's money. It is helpful to reassure your child that his money won't get lost and that he'll be able to get it out when he wants it. Let him know that he'll have a record of his money, either in a little passbook or in a statement that the bank will mail to him. He can put these important papers in a special file so he can keep track of how much money he has.

Since banks lend money to people for big things such as cars, homes, college educations, remodeling, and vacations, kids wonder if there will be enough money left over for them when they need to withdraw some for themselves. You can let the child know that banks have lots of money and that even if the bank makes some big loans, there will be enough money left over for him. You can tell him that our government guarantees his money will be returned to him. Point out the FDIC decal at the bank and tell him that the Federal Deposit Insurance Corporation was founded to insure depositors against loss.

You may not have even thought of making a point of taking your child to the bank. It's not as exciting as a visit to the firehouse, and it's difficult to make standing in line interesting, but you can use the opportunity to discuss the banking process. If you ask your friends for their memories of going to the bank, you'll hear such things as how "mysterious" the place seemed to be, how "clean and quiet" it was, what "fun" it was to go through the drive-in-window and get a lollipop. Cheri recalls the ritual of going with her mother into the depths of the bank to put things into the safe-deposit box:

> There were so many steep steps to go down that I felt I was entering another world. We'd have to wait a while before the security guard opened the door with bars on it. I felt like I was going into a jail. The whole business of signing in, handing over the key, following the guard into the vault, and being surrounded by all the metal boxes was very impressive. The door to the vault still amazes me. How gigantic it is even now that I'm five-foot-three. As a kid it was overpowering, and I couldn't figure out how bank robbers could blast their way through it.

The vault is usually a child's favorite part of the bank. Just being close to "all the money" is exciting. Even if you don't have a safe-deposit box, you can ask the guard to show your child the little rooms where people can sit in privacy to open their boxes. Just imagine with your child all the jewelry, coins, birth certificates, and other valuables that are stashed there. What treasures would your child want locked up?

The whole concept of security fascinates kids. Point out the overhead cameras and the thick Plexiglas window or grill that separates the tellers from the public and talk about the need for them. Ask what thoughts your child has about bank robbers and tell him yours.

When you take your child to the bank, explain what deposit and withdrawal slips are. Show your child how you fill them out and how you record your transactions. If you use the cash machine, show your child how it works and convey the attitude that this convenience is yours because you have money in the bank. Let your child see that you record your transaction in your checkbook and that you file your receipt in a safe place. If your child knows he will be responsible for keeping his own account, chances are good that he will assume this responsibility eagerly.

Make the whole process of saving fun. Let your child know that this is a challenge you'll help him meet. If the child understands the ideas and has good hands-on experiences while learning, he'll probably continue to be a saver throughout his lifetime.

To make the saving process even more rewarding, you might want to create a game board. Put spaces along the border to record weekly deposits and have some stickers handy to use as mini rewards for saving some money every fourth week. Make a fancy certificate that says or shows what the child wants and how much money has to be saved each week to accomplish the goal. Congratulate your child for reaching the mini goals and celebrate when the child makes the final payment. Display the certificate prominently and begin shopping.

SOME QUESTIONS FOR
THE BANKER

Not all banks are able to accommodate kids' accounts since the amounts are generally small, and banks, after all, are in business to make money. Finding out the bank's policy is essential. Most banks will accept a child's account providing that the parent has one with the bank. There might be a minimum that they ask you to keep in it, and you need to know if a minimum is required for the child's account also. Ask about the fees involved, which could eat up whatever interest the account might earn.

From an organizational standpoint, find out if your child will receive monthly or quarterly statements or if she'll have a passbook. Will she have a special identification card for transactions? When you open the account, will the banker explain interest to your child?

Are there other services available to the child, such as banking by mail, money-market accounts, and certificates of deposit?

If your bank won't allow your child to have an account, consider opening a custodial account with your name listed as custodian for your child. There are still Christmas Clubs for small savings, and don't forget Series EE Savings Bonds for a long-term savings plan. You get double the face value of the bond when it matures.

CHECKS

When you explain checks, you can include some of these thoughts. People get paid what is owed to them with a small piece of paper called a check. All checks say who is to get the money, how much, on what date, from what person, and from which bank. Checks are like money and can be used as long as there's enough money in the bank account. Every year, as many as twenty-billion checks are used in this country. The amount of money they add up to can be higher than eleven-trillion dollars! It's a good thing computers are available to keep track of all this subtracting from one account and adding to another.

Since checks are so valuable, kids need to know how to treat them safely. While you will probably want your child to be older before helping with the checkbook, you can nevertheless show how you fill out, endorse, record, and keep track of checks. Show her that you fill out the information needed in the register or on the check stub first, so you won't forget to record the check. Some other details to teach are to remember to use ink when writing a check, never to give a signed blank check to anybody, and to fill out the amount in such a way that no one could tamper with it to turn it into a larger amount.

At this stage, if your child likes arithmetic and is good at organizing, see if she's interested in doing the subtracting for the monthly bills. If you're lucky, she may even want to balance the checkbook. First, have your child put the checks mailed to you in numerical order. Then cross off each one that is listed on the bank statement. If you made deposits during the month or received interest, cross those off too. Subtract any service charges and the amounts of checks that you made out that haven't been cashed yet, and you ought to come up with the same amount that the bank did.

INTEREST

Interest is another subject that is difficult to explain, so the way to go about it is with as much simplicity as possible. For example, when people need money to buy supplies so they can get started in a business, they have to go to the bank for a loan. The banker lets the businessman put the loaned money into his checking account, but he charges a little extra for the use of the money. The extra money is called interest, and the businessman has to repay the bank a little every month until all the money is repaid.

Some of the money that the bank earns from loans goes to depositors to thank them for leaving their money in the bank. That money is called interest too. Banks make a profit when they lend to others at a higher rate than they pay depositors.

There are two kinds of interest, simple and compound. With simple interest, the bank pays you an amount at the end of the year. Compound interest allows your money to earn a little extra, since the bank will compute the interest by including the earned interest plus the deposit, called the principal. Banks compute interest annually, quarterly, monthly, and daily. The best deal is to have your money compounding daily. That means that as long as your money stays in the bank, it works for you every day to increase its value.

Before opening an account, it's important for your child to get the answers to two questions. One is to find out how often the bank will compound interest on the account, and the other is to get an idea of how much money will be left in the account at the end of a year after all the fees have been subtracted.

To impress your child with interest, try a little math. See how much money $100 can earn at six percent interest for one, two, and three years. Do the same for $1000. See how much you would have if you put in an additional $100 or $1000 each year. Don't forget that with compound interest the bank pays you for your principal as well as the interest the money earns. For one year, $100 will earn $6 and $1000 will earn $60. If you save $1000 every year for five years, you will have $597 if the bank pays six percent on it; and at the end of ten years, you'll have $13,972. Of course, there will be some taxes to pay, but the general idea is to show how money makes money.

LOANING MONEY TO FRIENDS

Children frequently borrow money from each other for snacks. Usually, the loans don't get repaid. This can be a source of irritation to a child who wants to maintain a friendship and fears that asking for his money back will jeopardize it. Unless some effort is made, either the money or the friendship will be lost. Small amounts usually are forgotten, but when there's a pattern either of your child banking others' treats or certain children repeatedly borrowing from yours, it's time to talk.

Ask your child for his thoughts on the matter. Does it appear that he makes friends by having extra money for them? If so, he needs some help to make friends in a different way. Everybody likes to be treated, but it's not necessary for maintaining friendships. Children, of course, are taken care of by parents, who pay for them, so kids may be emulating grown-ups to gain some status and recognition. It gets expensive and it usually doesn't feel so good after a while to bankroll others. Ask for your child's feelings about being a lender as well as about not being repaid.

A simple solution to a complicated problem is to have less money. When your child takes enough money for her own needs every day, she can be comfortable saying, "I don't have any extra money." Even if she does have some spare change, encourage her to say that she needs it for something later. If she's able to assert herself, she can say flat out that she only lends money for emergencies or that she doesn't like to lend money.

Repayment can be tricky, since kids don't have much money from the start. If your child is willing to forgive a small loan, she will have learned a valuable lesson. For those who do want to be repaid, some method has to be agreed upon. Help your child decide what minimum amount she would accept and how often the installments would have to be made. Support your child's businesslike voice and demeanor, and role-play with her about how she can talk to her friend about arranging for repayment.

Since banks charge interest on their loans, your child may want to also. You can explain that friends are not in business to make money from each other, so it's not really good to do this. However, in making a plan for repayment, your child could tell his friend that there will be a monetary penalty if he doesn't come through as agreed. The idea of imposing a consequence is better than a fee.

Another idea is to give the debtor a choice of either repaying the loan or doing something, such as a chore, to pay it off. Have the friend help rake leaves or bring homework home when your child is out sick.

For a truly chronic problem, honesty is best. Help your child say, "I don't want to lend you any more money because I can't afford to, since you don't pay me back." Where sizeable amounts are involved, you'll have to talk to the other child's parents.

When children use money to buy friendships, it is a way of showing their lack of self-esteem. The thought behind spending money on others or lending to a friend too often can also mean, "See how valuable I am to you as a friend, since I'm paying your way?" The problem is that these children may not feel that kids would be their friend any other way. Talk with your child to find out what she has to offer in a friendship instead of money. Role-play a scenario where your child is confronted with a generous friend who gives gifts, buys treats, and loans toys. See if your child can feel what it's like. Some feelings may be those of obligation, resentment, and guilt. Your child may feel indebted and trapped too. By putting your child in her friend's shoes, she'll be able to feel that what her intention was won't work. Instead of making a friend, she'll see that she makes her friend move away from her. Encourage your child to open up her genuine feelings of friendship instead of her pocketbook.

GOALS OF AGE NINE TO TEN

- Open a savings account.

- Have your child talk with a bank officer.

- Talk about concepts such as interest, compounding, deposits, withdrawals, checks, and accounts.

- Save for something that can be had in a short amount of time.

- Introduce your child to your checkbook and talk about how to organize it for balancing each month.

- Discuss lending or borrowing money from friends.

YOUR TEN TO ELEVEN YEAR OLD

ECONOMIC REALITIES AND YOUR FAMILY

THESE DAYS, FAMILIES HAVE UNDERGONE ENORMOUS CHANGES. There are millions of households headed by single, gay, and lesbian parents. Divorce and remarriage involve one out of five children. More than half of American mothers work out of the home. New families shuffled into new environments have problems galore, not the least of which is money. When there is remarriage or newly single status, the financial situation changes.

There are additional expenses, combined with a diminution of income in many circumstances. It's essential to let the kids know what the new circumstances are so they will have realistic expectations. Tell them what the changes will be and share your *general* financial picture with them, without scaring them or painting such a bleak scenario that they feel overwhelmed and unable to ask for anything.

If you are able to enlist their help, things can be better for everyone. For example, kids who help with the chores can save money that can be used for a movie or a pizza for the family. Maybe outside jobs are a possibility. Ask your children for suggestions as to what they feel they can contribute to help the family finances, but be sure their contribution is realistic.

Many parents who undergo these changes don't want to bother their kids about a new financial situation. This denial eventually backfires, since it's not possible to continue as if nothing has changed. Kids who aren't told about new money matters will be surprised eventually, as their standard of living changes. Contrary to common thought, nobody likes surprises, especially if they involve belt-tightening.

Kids want to know the truth. If they're included in a family-circle meeting, they'll feel their responsibility as a family member more. As a result, they'll pitch in to help and will make fewer demands.

By age ten, kids can take on some responsibility at home. It's good for them. How else will they learn to take care of themselves if they don't have opportunities? These days, kids can do the family marketing and get dinner going. Mom may not get home from work until late, and somebody has to pull things together. However, not all kids want responsibility; they like having everything done for them, but curtailing privileges usually works to get them to do their fair share.

In cases of remarriage, the standard of living may go up. Kids who helped out before may get the idea that they no longer have to do so. Parents who felt guilty asking their kids to pitch in may relax their expectations. Kids who profited from feeling responsibility may get the message that they don't have to anymore. You'll be smart to disavow them of this assumption.

With two parents there usually are two points of view about money. Divorce doesn't change that. The single most irksome thing that happens between divorced parents is sabotage. If one parent wants to teach the kids money management, and the other approves their requests for extra money, the kids will learn to "Dial for Dollars" rather than earn more. Bad habits get reinforced if a child learns that a parent will bail him out.

Gifts can be a problem too. In a remarriage situation where your children have step-siblings, it's possible to stir up a lot of jealousy if your ex is more generous than the other children's parent.

If possible, seek some agreement on the basics of how to handle such things as the allowance, gifts, and entertainment. A common complaint from divorced women who have custody of their kids is that they do all the work while the father gets to play with the kids. The "Disneyland Dad" treats the kids very well, while Mom scrapes by. There's a lot of resentment toward the parent who doesn't give gifts, too.

HOLIDAYS, GIFTS, AND VALUES

"Since my husband is unemployed and I'm worried about losing my job, this holiday season is not going to be a real cheery time," said Rosemary, who usually entertained her extended family. "The kids are getting smaller and fewer gifts, and I'm going to concentrate on the spiritual side of things this year. We'll take the kids to midnight mass and join the congregation in feeding the homeless. I want us to learn to count our blessings instead of our presents." She was frank with her family about the situation and found that everyone understood that the celebration would be different this year.

For many, it certainly is a new experience to have to put away the expectations of living up to prior holiday celebrations if money is in short supply. It's fine to feel angry and frustrated, but it's important to cope with, not deny the situation. It's still possible to have a warm and memorable holiday without spending a lot of money. Indeed, there are lessons about values and money that kids can learn because of hard economic times.

It's difficult to keep in mind that a holiday isn't only for shopping. The commercial aspects have taken over the spiritual ones, and there is much pressure to buy gifts for everyone. Yet we must remember to emphasize the importance of family togetherness, peace on earth, and cultural and religious traditions.

Gift giving should be done with thought and without breaking the bank. By age ten, kids take a real interest in exchanging gifts. They are aware of individual differences in people and can relate to their separate styles. If Junior is told to get Grandma "something nice," chances are he'll come up with a lovely and appropriate gift.

Children should be taught that the best thought behind a gift is, "I think you are special," and not how much something costs.

Even if a lot of money is spent on a gift to you, that doesn't mean that a matching one is in order when it's your turn to give. Some people don't like the feeling of obligation that a gift provokes—they tend to respond with gifts in kind, but not necessarily with kind feelings. Insecurity abounds about what constitutes good taste and what will be appreciated. Without knowing the unique interests and tastes of the people on the gift list, your choices may be of the generic, age-appropriate, one-size-fits-all variety.

Teach kids to think of the other person's style, favorite colors, and interests rather than considering how much money to spend on each person. The price of a gift is not a barometer of the relationship. It is hoped they can say thank you and smile even if they get something they don't like.

How often have you heard, "Oh, I have that," or seen a crestfallen face when a gift doesn't meet hopes or dreams? Encourage children to send thank-you notes for all gifts, no matter how disappointing or who the giver has been. Everyone wants to know their gift is appreciated and that you appreciate the time, energy, and thought that went into purchasing it.

Relatives and friends who live far away can't get the pleasure of watching children open their gifts, and if they don't get a thanks in the mail, they may be hurt as well as resentful.

Kids still prefer toys to clothes as gifts. These days it's tempting to give utilitarian gifts to fulfill that obligation and to clothe the kids at the same time. Consider combining the practical with something frivolous and fun, since these days we need both. Don't forget that after-Christmas sales can be helpful for filling in wardrobe holes.

When kids take tight economic times too hard, it's because they haven't been given all the facts. Tell them briefly how this year will be different for them. Include what they will have and what changes to expect. Let them know that just about everybody is being more careful with money these days. Saying, "We are comfortable," or "We have to be a little careful not to spend too much," are understandable words that won't raise anxiety. Finances can be conveyed in words rather than in actual monetary amounts. If pressed, you can say, "That's not information that would be helpful for you to know right now."

This age group also enjoys making things, so encourage them to do so. While they're at it, they can stockpile some things for Mother's Day and Father's Day too. Handmade items are more personal than store-bought things and are greatly appreciated. Kits that teach kids to make things are terrific gifts, and, in turn, the things they make can be presents for others.

Kids want to be involved in the decorating, baking, singing, shopping, cooking, and even cleanup. They like to cook and bake cookies. They don't need store-bought ornaments. If left without packaged entertainment, they just might learn how to entertain themselves.

If kids make cards or other things, and if these are given prominence in the home, kids feel pride in their skills. Wendy remembers making cards saying, "I love you," with macaroni letters. She smiles as she recalled the memory of them on display on the coffee table. Too many kids don't develop hobbies. They touch a lot of plastic, cardboard, and fake fur. So many just move their thumbs with video games instead of learning how to make things with their hands. It sounds old-fashioned, but there's a lot of pleasure in making things from scratch. Kids still like to make airplane and car models as well as needlepoint, knitting, and weaving projects.

EXPECTATIONS

"I need to know what your three favorite things are, and I'll surprise you with one of them," said a newly divorced mother to her children at holiday time, since she couldn't afford the fancy productions she presented to her family in the past. She didn't have to put a money limit on the amount to spend. Rather, she was honest and said, "Things are going to be simpler this year. Instead of having a big party, we're going to have a dinner just for us, and each of you can invite your best friend."

Kids don't necessarily expect bells, whistles, and fireworks. Often it's the parents who plant expectations in their kids' heads. The parental wish is to make the occasion special for the kids, but the big fear is that the kids won't be happy, no matter what they do. Maybe that is why so many parents overdo it.

Possessions don't make people happy, but they can make life more pleasant and nice. Real happiness comes from within, from sharing, doing things together, involving oneself in the whole process. It's always important to stress this with your children.

Without a doubt, the pile of presents under the tree can be a delight for kids. Kids don't have bills to pay, so they can really enjoy everything. The problem comes the next day when the toys that were so beautifully wrapped get broken, strewn about the room, and are never seen again. So many parents give too many gifts to kids. Kids experience it initially as a smorgasbord of goodies, but then what kids really want is not so much the presents—even though on the surface they will protest and say they do want them—they really want the *presence* of their parents.

GIVING GUILT

Ironically, there are many parents who moonlight to be able to afford the pile of presents so that their kids don't feel deprived at holiday time. They may be out of the house a lot as a result. Affluent parents with two paychecks also are unavailable, and there just isn't much quality time anymore. Out of guilt, these hardworking parents give too many gifts. Gifts may be a form of compensation for the dearth of family time.

It's hard to get away from guilt in situations where divorce, separation, conflicting priorities, and ambivalent feelings are concerned. Buying off guilt feelings is common, since it's easier to purchase things than provide what money can't buy.

Kids feel guilt too. If they don't get what they hope for, they may feel angry. It's dangerous to let that feeling out, so it simmers and sometimes finds its way out in unconstructive ways.

There's hype all around us. We have to plow through it and make our own traditions. Do what is meaningful for you and within your budget.

SPOILED OR MERELY INDULGED?

Parents worry about spoiling kids. It seems that the holiday season brings out The Gimmes. From Halloween through after-Christmas-sales shopping, the demands are constant. TV ads keep up the pressure, as one holiday follows another. Even if kids get what they want, they don't seem happy. The things so fervently lobbied for don't even get played with that much. Most parents don't want to deprive their youngsters, but they don't want to convey that the kids can have everything in sight either.

There is a natural urge to have new experiences, so it's understandable that all kids want everything and love to touch things in stores. They don't like to share and they aren't shy about asking for more and more. Sometimes what is important, however, is not the toy, but the joyful feeling the child gets when he actually gets his parents to buy things. Kids may be honing their negotiation skills to a fine point when they say they *must* have something. They're trying out their budding sense of power against yours, to see how much they can get.

Amy lobbied for a Swatch watch. She proclaimed that she "had to have one" Not a day went by without some comment or another about the urgency of having it. When her mother asked why she needed it so badly, Amy was unable to come up with any good reasons, especially since she already had a watch. "All the kids have them" was the best she could do.

If Amy's mother generally caves in and gives her what she wants, she will probably be faced with more requests. Another downside is that Amy won't learn when enough is enough. She'll think she can have it all, when the reality is that we all have limits. She'll grow to expect that she'll get what she wants. That sense of entitlement can last a lifetime. Also, she won't appreciate what she gets because she had no resistance to overcome, and Amy will become a spoiled child.

Indulgence is different from spoiling. Parents like to treat their children by indulging them every so often. It's a parental pleasure to be able to provide them with special things. The key factor is limits. Spoiled kids have no limits: Their parents seem to provide the works.

Ironically, one of the biggest problems parents face is affluence. The availability of things and the ability to buy them causes confusion and sometimes arguments. It is hard to say no to a child who wants an expensive item when there is money in the budget to cover it. Buying things for the sake of having them is fine, but there are more levels to explore in a purchase such as this.

For example, what do you teach your child when you gratify your child's wish? Is it that wishes do come true? If your child's wish is your command, then that child could go on to expect the same response from others. If others don't jump, then the child may be hard pressed to know what to do. When children's desires are gratified, their tolerance for frustration is thwarted. In the long run, making wishes come true may do more for you than for the child, if you're reaping good feelings and avoiding tension by saying yes.

But, you might say, "If you don't ask, you don't get." True enough; however, delivering the goods when asked sets up a pattern of expectation that can lead to asking for more and more. Eventually, the attitude of entitlement presents itself and can be extremely difficult to break. The kids feel, "it's due me." They expect more and more and show less and less appreciation. Saving or planning for the future becomes problematic because they haven't learned to be creative, patient, or resourceful. They don't learn how to set priorities if they get everything they want, so all things have the same importance. When parents meet all needs, children don't learn to provide for themselves. They don't learn what things cost, nor do they have a sense of being independent. For all of these reasons, it's important to put the brakes on runaway demands.

There are some things parents can do to undo or prevent spoiling. Saying no is still the best way to limit kids. Since kids appreciate things they've earned, help kids to make some money and to save it for something special. If your child doesn't have many friends, giving him toys and other playthings with the hope that other kids will take an interest in him won't work. The kids will come around to play with the new toys, but toys alone won't win your child any popularity contest. Help your child learn to be more social and less generous. Instead of rewarding him with new toys, find other ways to let him know you're proud of him. Too often, toys are used to keep kids in line, but bribes don't work. Sometimes kids will turn things around and demand toys because they've behaved. The bottom line is, spend more time than money on them.

CHARITY

Charity is part of the spirit of the holidays. If there is a Give-Away Box in your child's closet, this is a good time to take a look at what has been tossed into it. Good, outworn clothing and toys that are no longer appropriate can be bagged and donated to the Salvation Army or some other charity. The receipt for this can be used for a tax deduction.

As the holidays get closer, motivate kids to put their unused and outgrown things into the box by reminding them that new things need room. Some other child can enjoy the toys and clothing, and the belongings will continue to be useful or enjoyed. If you can involve your child in the process of gathering the things, packing them, and delivering them to a children's floor of a hospital, a Ronald McDonald House, or the pediatrician's office, he'll feel the appreciation from others and will learn the pleasure of giving.

GOALS OF AGE TEN TO ELEVEN

- **Discuss how economic realities affect your family.**

- **Emphasize family and cultural values.**

- **Put some perspective on the commercial aspects of the holiday season.**

- **Sensitize children to think of others when considering appropriate gifts.**

- **Insist on gracious receiving and thanking for presents.**

- **Involve kids in making things.**

- **Put some limits on kids' demands.**

YOUR ELEVEN TO TWELVE YEAR OLD

THE ENTREPRENEUR

THE FIFTH AND SIXTH GRADERS AT ONE ELEMENTARY SCHOOL in Texas have learned about business by starting one. They've produced and sold novelty items, run a snack stand, and have held fund-raising events such as pancake suppers. In a good year, they earn more than forty thousand dollars. This money goes for electronic equipment for the school, class trips to places as far away as the Caribbean, and investments such as certificates of deposit and money-market funds. They have learned to deal with the local bank by talking about a loan, cashing company checks, and making deposits.

When daily receipts fell about fifty percent, the kids learned how to stir up business. They marketed aggressively by mail to student leaders in other school districts by urging them to buy items that could be sold at their schools. The Texas Weather Rock was their leading product—if it's wet, it's raining, and if it's dry, it's not.

The kids learned firsthand about business headaches also. Their receipts had fallen, so they had to cut back on expenses, and that meant they needed to make a new budget. New business lines couldn't be developed. They had to eliminate their special monthly luncheon and work hard for more publicity. They learned about the ups and downs of the business cycle as they searched for problem-solving solutions.

Most schools don't offer practical, hands-on experience in starting your own business, so kids have to learn by doing it themselves. Those who accept the challenge may be more concerned with inventory control than more mundane math problems, but actual business experience can pay off with successes that make schoolwork more relevant.

Ten to eleven is a good age to encourage entrepreneurship in our children. As the world market increases, we can prepare our kids for the opportunities that will come. America has the most innovative business leaders in the world, but unless we educate and motivate our children, we won't be able to maintain our top position.

Since only two percent of America's population provides the jobs that support the other ninety-eight percent, it is in our best interest to stimulate more enterprises. As small businesses grow, more people will be hired, and that will help to keep America productive and successful.

Kids are capable of inventing products that can spawn enormous profits. Casey came up with a biodegradable golf tee that disintegrates instead of causing damage to mower blades. His product is now a family business with orders for ten million tees, wholesale priced at three cents each. Now there's a practical math problem that is truly worth doing.

When Ari was ten, he started selling kites from a tiny shop in upstate New York which he leased with his own savings. Now, at fifteen, he works after school and on weekends to keep his two stores going. The combined sales are expected to reach $160,000.

Jill spray paints designs on T-shirts and shorts that sell for ten to forty dollars. While her friends are her customers now, she's exploring the option of selling her shirts and shorts at local stores in Florida.

Valerie put together a study book for her fifth-grade spelling bee. She used her home computer to pull it together and then sold it to other schools. Now, she and her sisters have a mail-order business for products related to spelling bees, which sell to more than fifteen thousand school districts nationwide. That's one way to learn the ABCs of business.

One reason to encourage our children to become entrepreneurs is because a college degree is no longer a ticket to a good job. There are plenty of college graduates doing volunteer work, driving taxis, or going on for more diplomas because of economic conditions. It's no longer realistic to hope to get a job in a Fortune 500 company, climb the corporate ladder there, and retire with a pension and a gold watch. Job insecurity is more common.

Recession, inflation, down-sizing, and layoffs are causing people to go into their own businesses. It's time now to teach our children the basics of how to take an idea and nurture it into an enterprise that can be profitable. For a capitalist country, America leaves its kids woefully ignorant of what it takes to make a business grow.

The benefits, both educational and personal, of getting kids involved in some business activity are enormous. They get a picture of planning, researching, negotiating, and pricing. How to beat the competition becomes a part of their thought process. They develop skills at selling, marketing, bookkeeping, advertising, and public relations. If they can overcome buyers' objections and not take rejection to heart, they'll profit personally. Similarly, they'll grow by taking setbacks in stride and by learning from their mistakes. Not the least of the character benefits gained are reliability, honesty, and persistence.

There is a company called Kids Busines$ that puts out a kit with four explanatory booklets, a blank business plan, stationery, business cards, information on advertising and marketing, as well as an audio tape. It's for kids age ten to eighteen but could be helpful for anybody interested in starting a business. You can get information by calling 1–800–282–KIDS.

The mission of this company is to provide a self-study guide for kids who know little about business but who think they would like to start one. The booklets take the kids in a fun and uncomplicated way from understanding what a business is, how to get started, and what forms are necessary for organizing their enterprise, all the way to the basics of bookkeeping and public relations. After digesting the information in the booklets, kids fill out a business plan and see if their venture can work on paper before they invest in it.

WHAT MAKES AN ENTREPRENEUR?

Many books have been written about the kinds of personal qualities entrepreneurs must have to succeed. Confidence, ability to take risks, and vision are some that usually develop as an enterprise takes off. Initially, however, the budding entrepreneur actually may be a child who shows unusual intensity in something such as reading, learning new things on her own, or exhibiting a hefty amount of enthusiasm. There are kids who take pleasure in discovering something new and then following up on it without prompting. Their schoolwork may not be first class, but their ability to persist may be. Entrepreneurs come from all backgrounds, and their education isn't necessarily filled with degrees, but they do have to have the kind of passion and commitment that new ventures require. When these are evident in children, they need to be nurtured.

Another necessary ingredient for success as an entrepreneur is a willingness to go the extra mile. Kids usually do only what is required of them. They follow directions to satisfy the teacher or parent, and that's fine, but if they don't try for bonuses or extra credit, they miss out on learning the special quality of doing more than is expected. In any business, success comes to those who put a unique spin on something or go out of their way to help someone. "It's not my job to do that" isn't something an entrepreneur would say.

Compensation for some personal shortcoming is also found in the backgrounds of wildly successful entrepreneurs. Some people worked hard to overcome great prejudice regarding their race, religion, or a personal handicap. Their motivation to be accepted prompted them to feel they had to be super rich, powerful, and respected. They expend enormous energy making up for painful feelings and experiences.

If your child shows signs of becoming an entrepreneur, or even if there's interest in how business works, there are some basic things you can discuss. The concepts can help kids understand the world of business, as well as sensitizing and stimulating them.

WHAT KIDS NEED TO KNOW
ABOUT BUSINESS

Any business has to *fill a need*. If your child has a hobby or special skill, it might be turned into a money-making adventure, providing others will desire the product or service offered. A child who knows how to take pictures, fix bicycles, or take care of pets has marketable skills. An enterprising eleven-year-old boy started a business called Twinkle Toes. He advertised in his neighborhood newspaper that he'd collect businessmen's shoes on Fridays and have them shined and returned on Sunday.

Brandon calls himself a collector and a businessman. Ever since he started to collect PEZ candy dispensers when he was seven, he has spent his extra time pouring over price lists in *Toy Value Marketplace* and placing and responding to ads in *Antique Trader*. Because his parents are avid collectors, he got into the hobby easily and has a lot of fun searching for his special items at antique shows and flea markets. He now has about one hundred and fifty containers and is among about three-hundred PEZ collectors in the country, who wheel and deal by mail over these candy-dispensing toys. He answers three or four letters a week and uses his own money for making offers and taking options at auctions. His mother told him that, "collecting is not only something you can enjoy, but it's a way to make money to support yourself and have extra money." Brandon recommends that kids do serious collecting, because "they can have fun finding things at fairs and can talk about business with their parents." He even spoke before the graduate business students who attend his father's Principles of Economics class at the University of North Alabama.

Robbie and James are partners. Their business is collecting and selling golf balls that go askew from the local course. "We charge a dollar for four balls and golfers are happy to pay that, even though they may be getting some of their own back," Robbie said. He went on to say, "In the fall, we rake leaves and wash cars. We divide the profits and have double the fun because we do things together."

Some kids like to make things. Whether it's bird feeders or popcorn balls, there's probably a market for them. The trick is to find out what's needed and who wants it. It's necessary to do some preliminary research before getting started. For example, where are the homes that have trees for bird feeders in the neighborhood? If Halloween is approaching, popcorn balls could be great for trick-or-treat bags, so what stores might buy some? Would door-to-door selling after dinnertime work?

Once deciding on a product or service, it's important to get the word out to the potential customers. A *marketing strategy* promotes the business. Flyers can be helpful, but kids must plan how to distribute them. Can they be passed out to people on the street corner or slipped under neighbors' doors? The telephone is the best choice for selling some things, and mailings are better for others.

Advertising costs money, but small ads can work. Your child can find out what the community newspapers charge by calling them. If the child looks over the publication first, she'll be able to talk about such things as the size of the ad and how many words or spaces comprise a classified ad.

If advertising is too expensive, free publicity in the form of *public relations* might be an option. Your child can send a simple notice to the editors of the local papers announcing what she has and telling the essentials about it. Include a glossy black-and-white photograph of your child in action with her product or service, to improve the chance of getting a nice feature.

Learning about the *competition* is necessary. Your child may not be the first on the block to shovel snow or water lawns, but he can compete by doing it better, charging less, and providing more service. Kids are used to competing at school, in sports, and with siblings, so they'll catch onto the idea quickly. In business, many companies can compete successfully: One may be the biggest, but another can make the most money. There's room for more competitors, and there can be many winners. Your child can enjoy the rivalry that may develop from competing with other kids or even with neighborhood businesses.

Competition influences *pricing*. Kids may be tempted to charge too little or too much. They can find out what competitors charge by looking at ads or actually calling up others in their business and asking for prices. Where that isn't possible, children can figure a price range after considering such things as costs for supplies and equipment. The price must be high enough to make a profit and low enough to compete: If they price things too low, they'll lose money; and if it's too high, nobody will buy.

How prices are set depends on the way your child works. When kids do such things as baby-sitting and delivery services, working for a set hourly rate works best. Craft items are prices by the unit—$2.00 for each or $3.50 for two, for example. If your child takes on a big job such as planting flowers or cleaning out a garage, have him charge a flat fee. Of course, if your child lands a regular job, then a salary needs to be negotiated. When kids sell things such as magazine subscriptions, candy, or seeds, they may work on commission. Part of what they earn they get to keep, and the rest goes to the sponsoring company. Some people earn a salary and a commission.

Chuck Snyder is now the president of his own financial-planning organization, The American Group. Chuck had a series of service businesses as a kid and was able to put himself through college through various enterprises, such as buying used books and furniture from upper-classmen and selling them to freshmen. He developed a Valentine's Day business by selling boxes of candy to parents of co-eds and having friends deliver them. He didn't have to pay his helpers, because the guys did the job gladly as a way to meet girls. When he was on vacation at the seashore, he couldn't get a job, so he answered an ad for a chambermaid's position. The hotel had trouble finding females, so he was hired. He saw that this was a problem throughout the resort area, so he got jobs for other guys as chambermaids and collected fees for doing so. As if this weren't enough, he couldn't resist having his own business of washing and waxing cars to protect them from the salt spray. Of course, he had a couple of helpers do the actual work, while he made flyers and stuck them on the windshields of as many parked cars as he could find, especially those in the hotel parking lot.

With an enterprising father like Chuck, his twelve-year-old son had an inside track on how to make money in his own business. As a Boy Scout, he did some door-to-door sales of light bulbs and oven mitts, but this wasn't very exciting, and it was a lot of work. He found that a better item to sell was a discount coupon book from local merchants. For ten dollars, people could get seven-hundred to eight-hundred dollars' worth of money-saving coupons, and he could make four dollars on each book. On a good day, he earned as much as thirty-six dollars an hour. Now, that's motivating.

When your child does business with others, making a *contract* is a good idea. To avoid misunderstandings, have a clear agreement about what she'll do, how much she'll be paid, and when she'll receive her money. If she's offering some items to a store on consignment, get something in writing that states how the money will be divided between her and the shopkeeper, as well as when the money will be paid.

Of course, profits are the reason to go into business in the first place. If you can't make some extra money, there's not much use putting in the time and effort it takes to make a sale. *Profit* is what's left over after all the expenses and bills are paid.

Too many people go into business without making a *business plan*. A plan is like a picture of the business. It shows what is sold, how it will be done, and to whom. It lists the costs for starting and running the business, as well as giving some idea of what kind of profit may be made. After figuring out how much is needed to get going, it's important to think of how the money will be managed: There will be continuing financial needs that the business demands, and those should be in the budget. Unless kids take the time to project what their overhead and other expenses are, they may go out of business very quickly.

A *budget* includes all the costs of the business. The start-up costs are just the beginning. Add to those the costs of making, marketing, and selling the product. There may be expenses for gas and electricity, rent, supplies, ingredients, and even wages if someone helps to get the product ready for customers. After all of these items are taken into consideration, you must then figure out how many products or customers are necessary to make a profit. If a substantial amount of profit is predicted, don't celebrate until you figure out how much the taxes will be!

HOW TO NURTURE A BUDDING ENTREPRENEUR

When you see that your child has an idea for a business and some talent as an entrepreneur, you can be most helpful by being a guide and a sounding board. Don't encourage fantasies of fame and fortune, because they put too much pressure on your child. Thoughts of independence and self-sufficiency are fine, though, and will encourage your budding entrepreneur. You can also talk about the benefits of your child's product or service in order to encourage her, as well as provide useful information for flyers, advertisements, and simple press releases. Once your child can talk easily about these benefits, she'll be able to convey them to customers.

You can role-play sales interactions together. As kids rehearse their sales pitch with you, they'll envision what they may encounter with real customers and prepare themselves for their responses. You can also discuss why people might say no and plan what your child could say to counter some objections, including the finer points of her product or service. You can think up creative ways to advertise or, if she wants you to, drum up some business with friends, family, and colleagues. If you're available to type up business forms or pick up supplies, that can make life easier for your child. After all, nobody has to do everything in a business. If the business has a real future, you need to be aware of sales and income-tax consequences and maybe even liability insurance.

You can help with the bookkeeping. Set up a simple ledger with your child. Include the date, the record of the transaction, receipts receivable and payable, and have your child do the addition and subtraction.

Discussions about good business practices are excellent for character building. Such moral issues as keeping promises, telling the truth, and being reliable are inherent in these discussions. Focusing on the customer will pay off handsomely, so encourage your child to ask her customers questions about their needs and then to listen carefully. Perhaps she'll pick up some new ideas for improving her product or service. Help kids to plan ahead in order to have necessary supplies on hand and to avoid conflicts in their after-school schedule or homework responsibilities. After a job is done, encourage kids to ask for letters of recommendation that can be used for getting more business. Also, stress how important it is for them to tell their customers how much they are appreciated.

Another interesting learning experience is a visit to a location where goods are manufactured. Find out how much the product costs to make and what it sells for where it's made. Compare the price for this same item at gift shops or stores. That's what Bruce did when he took his daughter to an Indian reservation where all sorts of jewelry and crafts items were made. They talked with the people who did the polishing, setting, and stringing of beads to learn as much about the art as about the business of jewelry making. Later, they saw some of the Indian handiwork selling for twice as much in a boutique. This experience opened up a discussion about concepts such as wholesale, retail, markup, and overhead.

GOALS OF AGE ELEVEN TO TWELVE

- Become familiar with business concepts such as entre-preneurship, business plan, commission, and contract.

- Learn about setting prices and the competition.

- Talk about the benefits of products and services.

- Rehearse a sales pitch.

- Handle customers' objections.

- Learn the rudiments of budgeting, bookkeeping, market-ing, advertising, and public relations.

9

YOUR TWELVE TO THIRTEEN YEAR OLD

LEARNING ABOUT INVESTING

As Matthew blew out the candles on his birthday cake, it wasn't hard to know what his wish was. Most twelve year olds have music on their mind, and Matthew was no different.

Aunt Judy and Uncle Jerry heard of his yearning for the latest musical invention, and when Matthew opened his gift from them, he found a slip for several shares of Motorola Corporation. Why own a product when you can own part of the company? What a thoughtful gift, or so it seemed to everyone but Matthew, who looked a little disappointed. The confirmation slip for stock in a company was just a piece of paper to him. He wanted a record player, not a record of a transaction.

As statements came in for him, so did quarterly dividend checks.

They were for very small sums of money. At first he cashed them and laughed about them. Then he read about how he could re-invest his dividends automatically so that the money could go to-ward buying more shares of the stock. At one point, he commented wryly, "Oh, boy, I have enough for a tenth of a share."

But dividends aren't the reason to buy stock. It's the profit you make on the sale of the stock that counts. Eventually, Matthew did sell the stock and used his proceeds to buy a fancy portable compact-disc player and several CD's. That's how he learned the value of stock.

STOCKS

Matthew and several million other minors in America own stock kept in trust by an adult. Before recent tax laws went into effect, it was more advantageous for parents to have investments earning profits in a child's name. Now, it's just a good idea that can help kids learn how capitalism works. If kids have some shares of stock or some bonds, they are more apt to take an interest in their financial future.

If investing seems unreasonable or impossible for you and your child, start out with a pretend portfolio of stocks of fa-miliar companies listed in the stock tables as they appear in abbreviated form in your local newspaper. Favorite fast-food restaurants or clothing manufacturers could be a part of your portfolio, as well as companies that produce everyday items such as toothpaste, cleaning products, or canned foods. Check the labels of these products to get the names of the companies that make them. Decide on a pretend amount of money—maybe fifteen thousand dollars—and "buy" the chosen stocks according to how much they are listed for in the paper. [The price for each share can be multiplied by at least one hundred to get a decent portfolio going.]

Look over the stock quotations on the financial page together, to see the high and low for the day and the price of the stock for the day—the *close*. The *net change* shows the difference in closing price from yesterday's price to today's. Ask your child to figure out the closing price of the stock for the day before; that is, if the stock closed at 41⅜, and the net change was +⅜, the closing price from the day before was 41. Even if this information is listed in the paper, it's a good exercise to figure it out.

Sometimes there's a number after the name of the stock. That is the current *annual dividend*, the payment to stockholders per share of stock. For fun, ask your child to figure out how much would be earned for a hundred or more shares of some of these stocks. Stock prices are expressed in dollars and fractions of a dollar, so that ⅛ is 12½ cents, ½ is 50 cents, ¾ is 75 cents, and so forth. A stock selling at 45½ means $45.50 for each share.

People decide what companies to buy in different ways. Sometimes they like the products a company makes, or they read about new things a company plans to sell that are very desirable. Other times, they hear about trends in the news, the kinds of businesses that are doing well, or they read what experts recommend based on their research.

When you buy stock, you are actually buying a share of a business. It's a thrill for some kids to contemplate owning a part of Xerox or McDonalds. When they actually invest real money, they'll get notices from the company requesting their vote for board members and other decisions that affect the company. They'll be invited to meetings in big cities, and if they can't go to vote, they can mail in their vote on a proxy form. Even small shareholders are important. At times, they band together to offer their own opinion, which may be in disagreement with what the board members recommend. Kids can look over the annual reports, and even if they don't understand the news, they can get the gist of what happened to their company during the year by looking at the bottom line on the accounting page.

If kids like the idea of buying stock, they should understand that the object of the market is to buy stocks when they are low in price and then sell them when they go up to make a profit. It's easier to be aware of this strategy than to follow it! Even seasoned investors who follow the business news closely to know when it's a good time to buy or sell can lose money.

The daily ups and downs of the stock market are not as important as a long-range trend. It takes time to learn how to invest and time to make a profit from investments. Some people, when purchasing a stock, determine a number which they use as their selling price, such as thirty percent above what they paid for it. When the stock hits that number, they take the profit and invest in something else.

It's not a good idea to hold onto stocks for sentimental reasons. When you get emotional about investments, you can lose your perspective as well as your profits. Just because a favorite relative gave you a gift of some stock doesn't mean you have to consider it a family heirloom.

Similarly, becoming personally attached to stocks is a hazard. Saying "my" Disneyland or "my" Apple can make the stocks seem like a pet possession. But when a stock goes down and stays down, you must consider selling it. Leave your feelings out of investing so you won't lose your objectivity.

Some stocks just sit still with no movement at all. Some investors hold onto these "sloths" with the hope they'll increase in value even slightly so they can be cashed in for a graceful exit.

When stocks plummet in value, decide how long you'll hold on before cutting your loss. Anywhere from seven to fifteen percent of the actual stock's value is reasonable. Remember that by holding on and wanting to break even, you can lose out on other opportunities.

Surely the worst way to invest is to become reckless. Some people take bigger risks than they should to break even. What usually happens, though, is that they lose more money.

The person who places the order and helps you in other ways at a brokerage house is the stockbroker. The job of the broker is to facilitate trades between buyers and sellers. The broker gets a fee, a *commission*, for this work—don't forget to consider this when buying or selling your stock. It can range from two and a half to eight percent of whatever the stock costs to buy or sell. Even though there is this fee, which will come out of your profit, it should not influence whether you buy or sell. Don't forget to consider fees when your child is pretending to buy and sell as well.

To buy or sell stock, all you need is an account at a brokerage house and a telephone. You may want to set up an account at a discount brokerage house; and if you do, you will not have to pay commissions, or maybe substantially lower ones, since you will make your own decisions about what to buy and need no special advice. You can easily set up a joint account with your name and that of your child. If the investment is to be in your child's name, under the Uniform Gift to Minors Act, you can set up a custodian account. When one parent is the custodian, the child's Social Security number and date of birth appear on the account. At age eighteen the money belongs to the child, and the parent has no recourse. Some parents who don't know if their child will be fiscally responsible keep the investments in their own name.

Ask the broker or discount broker to tell you the *quote*, or price, on the stock of your choice. All brokers have a TV–like unit on their desk which has instant access to the financial information at the stock exchange. You'll hear what the last price was on the stock, and this is called *last*. *Bid* is the price some buyer is willing to pay for that particular stock, and *asked* is the lowest price at which someone out there is willing to sell the stock you're interested in. Depending on how much money you want to invest, tell the broker to buy so many shares *at the market*, which means that he should buy the stock at the best price when the order actually goes to the trading post at the exchange. The miracle of electronics makes trades from around the world possible in minutes.

Part of the investment process involves understanding risk. For some people, taking a risk is a sink-or-swim situation fraught with anxiety. The truth of the matter is that taking risks is not death defying, although there can be potential losses. Investors who start by testing financial waters one step at a time often find them pleasant enough to go into a little further.

Maintaining some control over risky situations helps to decrease worry. Calculated risks based on some preparation, knowledge, and successful experiences can help ease your way in preparing for any adventure. So it is with investing.

The degree of risk you're able to tolerate is a major factor. After all, you can lose money if your stock goes down beyond what you paid for it. Smaller companies with less of a track record are more risky to invest in than the so-called blue-chip stocks, but if they are growing rapidly, there will be good profits. In the game of poker, the blue chips cost more than the red or white ones, and that's how the most widely held stocks got their nickname. Investing in expensive stocks can be less risky, since they are from tried-and-true corporations, but they may not ring in the bigger profits that speculating can produce. Your child can invest in the pretend portfolio with long shots as well as more conservative choices in order to follow the difference in return.

MUTUAL FUNDS

Mutual funds are useful in limiting risk. Instead of investing in companies individually, you are allowed with a mutual fund to own a little bit of a group of companies. If one company in the fund doesn't do very well, it is hoped that others in it will. A stock fund allows you to spread your risk over numerous companies and offers some comfort in knowing that there are managers at the fund who will watch it carefully and make necessary adjustments. Mutual funds also allow you to add small amounts of money to your holdings when you can. Some will sell for a minimum of five hundred dollars and will accept as little as fifty dollars for future purchases. When you buy stocks, bonds, and mutual funds, you are hedging your bets with *diversification*. If stocks don't do well, usually your bonds will, so you won't lose all your investments.

Mutual funds don't move up or down in value much, so they are less exciting than stocks. They are less in need of attention, however. People who don't supervise their portfolios regularly are better off in mutual funds, because they are managed professionally. The managers have their own style of investing, so it's important to understand their philosophy and to think about whether you agree with them.

There are different types of mutual funds, which meet various goals and have greater or lesser degrees of risk. Income funds, such as those that include utilities, provide people with cash payments on a regular basis. These funds give a lower return than other stock funds.

Growth and income funds usually include larger companies that have been around for a long time. The object of these funds is to produce growth that will be greater than the rate of inflation and income that will offset the daily fluctuations of the stock market.

Growth funds are more risky. They concentrate on up-and-coming companies that show a fast rate of growth. Some portfolio managers like to take high risks for even greater rewards and will invest in aggressive growth funds.

Small capitalization funds, known as "Small Caps," invest in smaller companies that may be able to outperform many of the more mainstay corporations.

International funds invest in companies in foreign countries. How well they do depends on the political and economic conditions in the individual country as well as the fluctuations in its currency.

There are bond funds too. Money invested in them goes to paying off debts from the government, cities, states, and corporations. There are short, intermediate, and long-term bond funds. Some offer tax advantages, such as municipal bond funds.

Money-market funds have the lowest risk and are the most liquid. It is helpful to have one of these funds to park money for emergencies or to keep ready cash, for other investment opportunities. The rate of return is lower for this type of fund than for other funds, but it offers conveniences such as check-writing privileges and many have tax advantages.

Some mutual funds carry *loads*, which means *commission*, and others are *no-load funds*. When you buy funds from a brokerage house, bank, insurance company, or from financial experts who work on commission, you will pay four to eight-and-a-half percent for the service. However, if you buy a fund directly from the mutual-fund management company, you can avoid the extra fee. You can call these companies toll-free for more information and applications.

Your child can call or write for information on stocks or mutual funds. The prospectus and annual reports tell how healthy the companies are. Many advertisements in the business section of the daily paper encourage inquiries. The information is written in English, but it can be daunting. You and your child can look through the material to see what you can understand without having a master's degree in business administration. Look for what is in the portfolio, how it's traded, who is in charge, and what the performance has been over the last five years. What you want to convey to your child is that investigating investments is important and necessary to minimize risk.

Check out more than the company's profits. See how many shares are in the company and how the earnings per share stack up. There's a big difference between a company that earned one million dollars with one million shares and a company that earned the same amount of money, but with ten million shares.

As with any investment, it takes time for it to grow, so parents who hope to pay for such things as college expenses are advised to begin an investment program as early as possible. In addition to mutual funds, some popular ways to invest include government savings bonds, municipal bonds, and zero-coupon bonds. These investments are conservative and are for the risk-averse, but their return is lower than equity funds that feature stocks.

U.S. Savings Bonds can be bought by mail at banks and other institutions qualified to issue them for amounts from twenty-five to five thousand dollars. Regular saving through the payroll savings plan offered by many employers helps parents accumulate small amounts of money that add up to a sizable amount over time. If savings bonds are used for educational purposes after being held for five years or longer, the interest is tax free. There are rules about family income and how the educational benefit works, which you can request from the Office of Public Affairs, U.S. Savings Bonds Division, Washington, DC 20226. Call your Internal Revenue Service district office for questions you have about record-keeping requirements and taxes.

RECORD KEEPING

It's important to keep records of investments. The notices that come in the mail, which tell you the price you bought a stock for, need to be kept in a safe place. When you sell the investment, you will be taxed on the profit you made. Each month, the brokerage house will send you a statement of how much money you made or lost that month. Keep handy a list of the stocks, bonds, or funds, with their abbreviations and the price you paid for them, for quick reference.

As you and your child go through the motions with your pretend portfolio, you'll be learning valuable lessons. Not only will you be aware of how businesses operate, but you'll be on the lookout for the products in your portfolio. Maybe your purchasing patterns will reflect this too. It's fun to purchase and use the products of the company in which you own stock. Of course, the big lessons are those of risk and reward. Kids will be able to practice math skills as they integrate concepts of economics, be encouraged to save some money, invest it, and add to their investment as they get older. Playing the stock market—even without a real money investment—is challenging and fascinating to the eleven to twelve year old.

COINS

Rare coins offer another avenue for investing. There are more than sixteen million collectors and investors who enjoy owning and learning about coins. This hobby can prove to be a high-yield and low-risk investment. The important thing to know about rare coins is that the supply diminishes as people hold onto their collections. With fewer coins traded, their value increases. However, as with stocks, coins are *liquid* investments. They can be sold easily to dealers and brokers.

Our government sells new coins through the Bureau of the Mint. The coins for collectors are never meant to be used. They are called "proof coins" and come in special annual sets where you get shiny unused coins in all denominations. They make nice gifts for kids. If they're held for the long haul, they can be good investments. If you want to buy proof sets from previous years, you have to go through a dealer. As with anything else, beware of anyone who offers you a "fantastic bargain." Your child's name can be added to a mailing list to receive information on future sets. Just write to: Director of the Mint, 55 Mint Street, San Francisco, CA 94175.

The condition of coins is a major factor in determining value. Scratches and other signs of wear lower the value. The new and protected proofs are in the best category, followed by uncirculated, extremely fine, fine, very good, good, and fair. Even though you may come upon some coins that are grungy in appearance, the best advice is not to clean them. Believe it or not, a cleaned coin is lower in value than a dirty one.

Grading is very important if you're collecting investment-level coins. The Sheldon Numerical Grading Scale, or MS Grading, goes from 1 to 70. The higher the number the better. MS Grades 60 through 70 apply to uncirculated coins, and those are the ones considered best for investment.

If profit is not your child's main consideration, coins that are extremely affordable, such as Washington quarters, can be purchased for one or two dollars. They are collected primarily for personal enjoyment. Coins that feature presidential likenesses, or five-coin sets from the ten different mints, are also good collection goals. Beyond the beauty of the coins, they inspire an interest in history.

Another relatively inexpensive but enjoyable way to collect coins is to buy rolls of unminted coins. You can get these from the Bureau of the Mint. For example, a roll of fifty dimes from 1949 sold for $5 then and is worth $2,375 today. A roll of ten Kennedy half dollars from 1964 was worth $5 then and $80 now. Also, from time to time, the U.S. Mint comes out with special coins to celebrate historically important events. These coins are called "commemoratives." They usually have low mintage, so they are popular with collectors.

A *Guide Book of U.S. Coins*, popularly called The Red Book, is the basic guide to coin prices. It is published by Western Publishing Company, Racine, WA 53404, and costs about $8.95.

STAMPS

Stamp collecting can also be enjoyable as well as profitable. There are over twenty million stamp collectors in this country. All of them are potential buyers and sellers of stamps. Buying from them can get your child started in this hobby, which some children turn into a business. The growing number of collectors bodes well for stamp collecting as an investment.

If you and your child look into this interesting world together, it can be beneficial to you both. It can be a treasure hunt to track down "blue chips," commemoratives, and oldies but goodies. You can talk and read about them as well as exchange them with others. It's a good long-term togetherness project.

Once you have the equipment of stamp collecting—an album (two dollars to two hundred dollars), tongs, hinges, glassine envelopes, watermark detector, and magnifying glass—you're ready to begin. The Scott Publishing Company, P.O. Box 828, Sidney, OH 45365, offers a wide assortment of albums and a monthly stamp journal for serious collectors.

Stamps can be bought from dealers at retail and sold to them at wholesale prices, but it's more fun to be in touch with other collectors. It's more profitable, too, since you can sell your stamps to them at the retail price. Collectors advertise in magazines and newspapers, such as *Linn's Stamp News* (a weekly), P.O. Box 29, Sidney, OH 45365, and *Scott's Stamp Monthly*, P.O. Box 828, Sidney, OH 45365. You might also look for stamp clubs in your area.

By looking over several issues of stamp-collecting magazines, you can compare the prices on similar stamps. With your help, children can prepare a small ad and even make the telephone call to find out the advertising rates. They can look up and call dealers in the Yellow Pages of the telephone book to find out the wholesale price (forty to ninety percent of the retail value). This can be an excellent demonstration of how people in business make a profit, and they'll learn what *retail* and *wholesale* mean.

Some stamps have skyrocketed in value over the years. A wildly successful story is the one about a man who bought a sheet of one hundred airmail twenty-four cent stamps and noticed that the picture of the airplane was printed upside down. This was a rare mistake, and he was able to cash in on it. In just a few days he sold the stamps for fifteen thousand dollars. Today, a single stamp from that sheet costs fifty thousand dollars.

Stamps can be found at flea markets, antique fairs, and maybe in your parents' attic. Old postcards and letters might have valuable stamps on them. Collections are sold at auction houses. If possible, go to them and make some bids. That can be the most exciting part of this hobby. Your child will also learn that old things are valuable and that time is important in investing.

The U.S. Postal Service, Philatelic Sales Division, Washington, DC 20265, will put you on the mailing list for commemorative stamps. The government puts out some low-cost books on stamps, and you can get information by writing to the Superintendent of Documents, Government Printing Office, Washington, DC 20402, or check your local post office.

Even if the size or value of the collection remains on the moderate side, the experience of sharing this hobby is priceless. This is something you and your child can share, which can have lasting value in terms of quality time and pleasant memories. Who knows, you might even find the most valuable stamp in the world—the British Guiana one-cent Magenta printed in 1856. It's now worth three hundred thousand dollars!

GOALS OF AGE
TWELVE TO THIRTEEN

- **Learn a little about investing in stocks, bonds, mutual funds, coins, and stamps.**

- **Make a pretend portfolio and follow some stocks.**

- **Look at the financial page for news about familiar companies.**

- **Read the stock tables.**

- **Understand jargon such as shares, dividends, mutual funds, risk, reward, prospectus, commission, bid, and asked.**

- **Learn to keep financial records.**

- **Consider collecting coins or stamps for pleasure and profit.**

10

YOUR THIRTEEN TO FOURTEEN YEAR OLD

CHALLENGES OF ADOLESCENCE AND SPENDING

PARENTS ARE FREQUENTLY IN OPPOSITION TO KIDS BUT MOST prevalently during adolescence. The necessity for kids to express their separateness and closeness, dependence and independence, conformity and individuality all at the same time can be emotionally draining for the entire family. There are at least four targets teens use to create distance from parents whenever they want it: music, cosmetics, hair, and clothing. Money makes all of these things possible, so fights over expenditures on these items are common.

Teens have to pull away from the family to find out who they are, what they want to wear, who they want to be, how they want to be perceived, and what they want to keep or throw out from what they've learned so far from their experiences at home. This is why they experiment with outrageous clothing, criticize everything you do, and stay in their rooms for hours on end. They don't want to be told what to do or be asked to be accountable for their actions. They don't want you to know their business or their thoughts. They want distance to figure out what they feel, hope, and believe. They want your support while they go out on their own limb. In fact, picturing this image will help you remember how difficult adolescence is, especially during those times when you try to be supportive and your child shuts you out.

Teens are still economically dependent and do have to live with you for a while. As they get older, they make more money, but they don't make enough to live on their own. The dilemma parents face is how to be helpful to these kids so eventually they can be on their own. This is hard to do since the kids won't give you the time of day, let alone allow you into their life. Teens today spend nearly everything they earn, so, unless their earning abilities or savings improve over time, they'll be living it up while living at home. Money surely provides a measure of independence, but as long as they're under your roof, they're dependent on you.

Teens spend their money on such things as telephone answering machines, movies, clothes, jewelry, sporting gear, and food. If they earn enough money, they might get gold jewelry, leather coats, pump sneakers, and multigear bikes. Many buy roller blades, CD players, tapes, CD's, tickets to rock concerts, cars, tennis racquets, and designer sunglasses. You'd be surprised how many kids spend money on trips to Europe, cross-country jaunts, or airplane tickets to visit their first love after they get to college. Guitars, keyboards, transistor radios, and microwave ovens are sold by the thousands to affluent adolescents. The amount of money that's spent on haircuts, perms, shampoos, and conditioners runs into the billions.

Some adolescents who don't have the money to spend may shoplift. The estimated amount of goods stolen annually by teens amounts to millions of dollars—perhaps into the billions. (See more about shoplifting in Part Three.)

FAMILY STYLES

Authoritarian or traditional types of parents will say, "While you're living in our home, you abide by our rules." This goes for how the children spend money, too. These parents don't let their kids carry around a lot of money. They might say, "When you earn beyond X amount of money, the rest goes into the bank." The parents decide what happens to their child's earnings in these cases. They say such things as, "I let her have only so much money," or "I don't believe in spending money on junk food, so I don't let her have money for that." The kids don't have much say in making decisions here either.

On the other side of the coin are the laissez-faire families, which are more prevalent as more parents work and are less involved in the details of daily life at home. So many parents don't have the time or energy to keep an eye on what their kids earn or buy. In this situation, there is little limit-setting. Basically, teens are being their own parents and are not sure how to do it. Some are too cautious and others throw caution to the wind. There are many children who spend impulsively, borrow money from their friends, or work too many hours to be able to function well at school the next day.

The ideal family style is a balance, whereby parents can talk to teens about working, setting goals, and planning expenditures. They can renegotiate the allowance and discuss the fine points of managing the new discretionary income a part-time job provides. Ultimately, it would be wonderful to achieve this balance without being controlling or bringing into the money discussion other major concerns adolescents have.

Until the twentieth century, kids had to work to help the family survive economically. It was expected that children would work to make contributions to the household budget. Never before in the history of the world have children had as much money of their own to spend as they do now.

Growing up in affluence gives children an odd perspective. They take luxuries for granted and, in fact, consider them necessities. Stylish clothes, new shoes, summer camp, and entertainment are things many kids couldn't imagine doing without. Often they don't have to, either, since baby-sitters in New York City now get as much as nine dollars an hour, teens who work in fast-food restaurants can get overtime, and delivery boys get dollar tips or more for bringing home the groceries or delivering some Chinese food. A gang of kids can chip in for a pizza. It doesn't take much money to maintain a moderate teen life-style, but when underlying emotional needs stimulate certain behavior that takes money, the parent needs to step in to monitor the situation.

TEENAGE MONEY STYLES

Kids, by their teens, generally have their own money style. While money provides an overall sense of independence, there are several specific types of money handlers: the savers, the competitors or adventurers, and the ingratiators.

The savers are goal oriented. When asked why they want to work, for example, they'll answer, "for college" or "for a car." They think of the future perhaps more than the present. When they get money, they hold onto it. As a result, they tend to make do with what they have rather than buying new things. When they get something new, It's regarded as a good buy, perhaps a bargain, and certainly something that will get a lot of use.

The adventurers or competitors are those who want to be leaders. These are the "cool" kids who set new trends. They are first in line to get the latest and the greatest. They compete for dominance in their circle of friends, whether they are actively competing on a playing field or vying for attention in other ways. Those who are adventurers are the ones who do unusual things. For example, some go on bike trips in Europe, others ride motorcycles, many like such things as parachuting and parasailing. They use their money for new experiences that are exciting. It costs money to maintain prestige and status; whether it's weight lifting, wrestling, or white-water rafting, every sport needs a complete outfit with shoes to match.

More girls are ingratiators than adventurers. They want to be liked, so they'll spend their money to make themselves more desirable, or in an effort to improve friendships they'll do favors and give gifts. They'll also put their money toward social activities, clubs, and clothing that reflects their belonging in their own social group. These are the kids you will find at the mall, and they tend to be impulsive spenders and live in the present. Next week is too far away to worry about, so as long as they have money now, they're ready to play.

CHANGES IN THE ALLOWANCE

If you've been giving your child an allowance, the challenge of adolescent expenditures will determine how to renegotiate it. If hobbies have taken a serious turn and supplies or equipment need to be upgraded, then it will be time to decide who pays for what and how much. Take into consideration all the expenses the teen will be responsible for handling and include some extra for discretionary spending, just as you did with the first allowance. Teens' expenses go up, since they include more social activities, more expensive gifts, and more miscellaneous things such as yearbooks, souvenirs, dues, and social weekends. Teens expect that you will bear the cost of feeding and clothing them, but you might consider putting a cap on these givens, as well.

Roberta shopped with her daughter, Sandra, every August for new school clothes, so she had a ballpark figure of what was spent each year. When her daughter made it clear that she wanted to shop by herself, Roberta told her the amount of money she would contribute, and if that didn't cover her purchases, Sandra would either pay for or forgo the extra items. This plan gave the child the independence to do her own selecting while the mother maintained some limits. It also enabled Sandra to determine which clothing items were really important to her and not just the latest fad which she could live without.

Since teens are also attracted to high-priced electronics, especially tape recorders, Walkmans, and CD players, some means for buying them is necessary. If parents don't want to pay for these in full, it's up to the teen to be resourceful through some kind of work or by saving in order to buy them.

Teens know the prices of items they crave. They've strolled many miles in the aisles at malls. They've perused catalogues for years, and they've shopped independently. They're pretty sophisticated about how much things cost, the "out-go," but they may be in the dark about the value of a dollar or ten, the "income." It can be an eye opener for teens to whip out their calculators and take over the family checkbook for a while to get a feel for managing real money. Next to getting a job of their own to experience just how long it takes to earn enough money for something substantial, experiencing the family budget can be a big dose of reality, especially for kids who tend to spend more than they ought to at times.

HOW TO TALK TO YOUR TEEN ABOUT EXPENDITURES

Andrea wants to perm her hair, and you hate the idea. Jerry spends a couple of dollars a day playing video games after school, and you think this is a waste of time and money. Peter buys tapes of every rock band in existence, and you think that's ludicrous. You know if you express your feelings, you'll likely start World War III. The more you speak up and voice displeasure, the more it seems your teen will continue to do what you don't like. On the other hand, standing by helplessly and observing the results of the shopping sprees builds up tension.

Remember the four areas in which teen/parental tensions are fueled: hair, cosmetics, clothing, and music. Let's take the permed hair. What you can do is talk to your teen about what she's considering doing. You may think your daughter is making a big mistake, and maybe she is, but her behavior with her hair is symbolic of what's going on inside her head. Is she self-conscious about her looks? Is she feeling out of control and wants to feel she can effect a change? Does she want to be part of a certain group? Ask her what gave her the idea, how she'd like to look, and why. You can also let her know that she'll have to pay for the perm herself, which might help her decide how important it is to her, but address the underlying issues as well.

When video games take up too much time and money, it's important to understand what's going on to make this activity so involving. Some kids seem drawn to the machines as if some magnetic force is pulling them. The concentration and tension build up during the game and the release is relaxing, so it's a good bet that budding hormones have a big part to play in the game too. Not only does the playing have sexual parallels, but it allows the teen to work off his urges in a socially acceptable way. Games also allow a safe way to unleash some aggression. When you have a tough, cruel world to deal with, it's much easier to have it at arm's length and scaled down to TV–screen size. Since power and control are major issues for teens, games give them a semblance of it when they zap and bleep enemies and monsters. The sense of competence may be shaky on the academic or athletic front, but when a high score gets electronically entered for all to see, it feels extremely good. Some kids have marvelous eye-hand coordination, so their thumbs work well even if their running, catching, or throwing skills need practice. Persistence and repetition improve one's score, so some children feel better about themselves when they can make it happen. It may be more doable to improve a score than a grade at school. Mastering a graphic universe can make a teen feel a sense of competence that is missing in other areas of his life. How the teen performs at a video game may reflect how he sees himself. Sometimes he's a winner and other times he's a loser. As these are only games, the teen's reputation is not at risk for long. Where there's a quarter, there's hope of doing well again.

When you talk to your teen about your concern that he's spending too much time and money at games, you will have to be patient in order to understand his reasons. He may not be able to tell you why he plays so much, since a lot of what he's doing is either unconscious or tough to talk about in the first place. Sexual and aggressive urges, wishes for competence and control, and attempts at improving one's self-image through mechanical means are some possible things to be aware of and to talk about as you learn more by listening. If you've observed some seemingly unrelated things going on in his life, you can draw him out about them, and then, if you see a connection, tell him your thoughts and watch his reaction to see if you're right.

When Peter first started buying audio tapes and records of his favorite bands, it seemed like a normal thing for a teen to do. Teens go to the favorite music store and browse until they choose as many selections as their budget will bear. Gift certificates are a favorite present, and cashing them in can get a collection off the ground.

Music is a ready outlet for rebellion. Parents usually hate the music, can't understand the words, and wince at the volume kids insist is central to the full enjoyment of it all. By listening closely to the words, you'll get an earful of what teens' concerns are. Sexual innuendo, code words for drugs, wishes for love, dependence, and battle cries of independence are some of the favorite subjects. The beat and the atmosphere of rock can be grating and soothing at the same time. The combination of intellectual interest in the compositions and the uninhibitedness of performers grabs teens and gets them to spend their money willingly. It's easy to buy some music and be the first on the block to tell others about your latest discovery. If being a leader is important to your teen, perhaps you can discuss less expensive ways to set a trend.

When kids spend all their money on music, they may not be acting in their own best interest. You might give a little guidance toward future purchases, as a way of curbing what seems to be too much spending too fast. Remind kids that if they don't save some money, they won't be able to upgrade their equipment or see a concert. When you hear your child talking about the sound he gets from his system, you could say something like, "Have you thought about how you are going to buy better speakers?" This will help sensitize your child to the future.

Planning and thinking ahead helps kids learn to put off spending. The teens who don't save will learn through their own mistakes eventually, but it can be a costly lesson. Still, if they get the message on their own, it's better than having you nag, demand, or threaten. Your job is to encourage them to work in order to pay for their expenditures, allow them to make mistakes, and help them be responsible for paying bills they acquire.

These principles apply, whether your child is working and has extra money or has only an allowance and gifts as income. As long as he's not spending money on drugs, alcohol, or anything else dangerous or illegal, the money your child earns ought to belong to him to do with as he wishes. By exploring underlying issues that are reflected in unhealthy spending patterns, you can determine if your child is lonely, angry, or even unsure of what else he can do with his money. Perhaps he is in need of a friend to visit or someone to go to the movies with; or maybe unhealthy spending acts as a salve to shut out thoughts about school or other problems. Solving underlying issues can resolve improper spending habits.

GOALS OF AGE THIRTEEN TO FOURTEEN

- **Avoid power issues over money with your teen.**

- **Recognize the main teen issues: separation/closeness, dependence/independence, and conformity/individuality.**

- **Prepare for independent purchasing.**

- **Moderate teen money styles and adjust the allowance.**

- **Understand what spending means from an emotional viewpoint.**

11

YOUR FOURTEEN TO FIFTEEN YEAR OLD

ERIC WAS ABOUT FOURTEEN WHEN A NEW LAW CAME INTO EF-fect in New York that refunded five cents for each soda can brought back to the store for recycling. I thought that seemed an easy way for a teen to earn a few extra dollars. When we were taking a walk in Central Park, I brought up the subject and wondered what he thought of collecting some cans to try out the idea. He liked it, so we found a relatively clean plastic bag in one of the trash cans and began a treasure hunt. He picked up a big stick and made it pointed on one end so he could fish out the cans without touching them.

We walked throughout the park, poking around in the garbage cans, and had a lot of laughs. It was a peculiar experience for me, and I did hope that I wouldn't bump into anyone I knew, but Eric and I really enjoyed this offbeat project.

The money Eric earned stimulated him to come up with his own business idea. He decided to collect cans from our apartment building, which is a thirty-two-story skyscraper with nearly two hundred apartments in it. I could see Eric's excitement as he made up a flyer detailing his recycling business. After he made copies of it, I helped him slip these notices under our neighbors' doors.

Next, he bought new plastic bags with handles on them that could be slipped over doorknobs. Once a week at a scheduled time, he collected a full bag of cans from the neighbors' doors and left a fresh bag for the following week's collection.

In addition to the extra money Eric earned, he became more ecologically aware, developed a sense of responsibility, and experienced customer service firsthand, since he had frequent contact with some neighbors. He learned about overhead, too, and when he saw that the cost of the new bags was substantial, he had to decide whether to expand his can-collection business or settle for less profit.

BENEFITS OF WORKING

Teens like having extra money. It makes them feel independent and gives them purchasing power. They should be able to buy what they choose and spend their money when they want. They also seem to appreciate what they buy when the money they spend is their own. And if a teen is able to earn his own money, he will ask less from his parents.

Of course, schoolwork is still the child's primary responsibility, but a part-time job can provide many additional benefits. Responsibility is one. When kids work, they are held accountable for what they do. It is a big responsibility to take care of somebody else's affairs, be at work on time, dress properly, and act professionally. Many kids don't learn these lessons until they have a job.

Teens' self-esteem and self-confidence will grow as they follow through on different jobs or as they create their own money-making ventures. Brainstorming ways of earning money can be very beneficial and will help your teen maximize her own interests, hobbies, and skills.

As kids help others they will be less self-centered, since they will be involving themselves in the lives of others and gain experience outside the family. This can be a real eye-opener for teens whose lives are too sheltered.

Teens who work at part-time jobs also learn that, even if they make a mistake, it is necessary to keep trying. Perhaps they will even talk to you about their mistakes and react to their failures in constructive ways, but some kids like to work out their own problems, so don't be surprised if they don't tell you much.

As the part-time job becomes routine, the teenager will learn how to manage time better, too. She will have to make decisions about when to study and how to be more efficient with homework. Such planning ahead and time management are also transferable skills for future jobs.

There are many reasons, besides money, that prompt kids to take on outside jobs. Maryanne felt restless and bored, got into fights with her mother, and decided to baby-sit in order to get out of the house. Adam became a busboy at a fast-food restaurant to help a cousin; then he realized he like to cook and was able to experience the start of what turned into a career. Mario was concerned about his grandmother, so he started delivering newspapers in order to be able to give her extra money every week, as well as to help his little brother take piano lessons. Janet knew her blind neighbor couldn't read the weekly letters she received from a sister who lived in another state, so she made an arrangement to become a reader and now makes trips to the library for her neighbor as well.

Regardless of their original reason for taking on the job, each of these teens was able to receive the benefits of working, even if they were not legally of age to be hired by a corporation.

INDULGENCE CAN BE DEPRIVING

If you are still concerned about your teenager obtaining a part-time job, keep in mind that if you continue to provide all material things, you are doing more of a disservice to your teen than you realize. When successful people talk about their secrets of accomplishment, they frequently point to their own hard work in building up a business from nothing, or that they learned the benefits of working at various jobs at an early age. Don't deprive your kids of the personal satisfaction of succeeding on their own terms. Strength of character as well as emotional security are often more easily acquired outside the family circle.

If you see yourself as the provider of all material things, are you doing it to be loved, to keep the peace in the family, or to be in control of the finances? None of these reasons is in the best interest of your teenager, who will only come to resent your generosity and not learn to appreciate what they earn from their own efforts.

Too often we hear stories of the child who "had it all" and still threw it away by getting into some kind of trouble—emotional, physical, or legal. Encourage children to pursue their personal goals, earn money if those goals require it, and become a productive member of society as soon as they are able. For more advice about encouraging your child to work, see page 90, "Parents' Needs versus Children's Needs."

PARENTS AS EMPLOYERS

It's difficult for parents to be employers, since kids often have ambivalent feelings toward their own parents, and your teen might do better working for someone else, perhaps a neighbor or friend. Maybe you can employ a teen and have his parents hire yours. Regardless of how you go about hiring a teen, however, you must be sure at all times to approach the employment as a job.

Chores are different from jobs. Look for things at home that can be viewed as a real job, and handle your child as an employee. Supervise, inspect, correct, and encourage. Perfection doesn't exist, so don't expect too much or your teen could quit in frustration. If the child can stick with something until he's satisfied with it or try again if he fails, that's a marvelous beginning. You may show him how to do something, but, remember, if he does the job his way and it gets done, that's fine. Doing the job at an agreed-upon time and for an agreed-upon amount of money is part of the deal. In the case where a child's reliability hasn't been tested, having a job at home can be a helpful way to get him ready for the job market. Kids can paint walls and fences, refinish furniture, steam-clean carpets, sew new covers for throw pillows, and plant next spring's tulip bulbs for extra money.

A lot of children earn money in the home from the time they're quite young. Some help out with the family business or baby-sit for their younger brothers and sisters. Some deliver food, have paper routes, and walk dogs to earn extra cash. Dottie made doll accessories, Bob shoveled snow, Rachel helped her aunt cater a tea by making the sandwiches and scones. Polly grew tomatoes in the backyard. Beth made out monthly checks for her grandmother, who couldn't see very well.

Often, after performing these jobs for a parent, kids can be very resourceful and take their services out into the neighborhood. Washing windows or cars, sitting plants or pets, making or baking specialty foods, cleaning attics, mowing lawns, or weeding flower beds are all money-making ventures that can be learned at home and then marketed to the neighbors.

Elderly people often need errands run, medication dispensed, or groceries picked up. Some kids are proficient enough with computers to teach adults how to use them. By age fourteen, those kids who want to make extra money can do so if they have the right attitude, as well as encouragement from you.

Since we are talking about fourteen to fifteen year olds, you will most likely be paying them in cash and not paying taxes or benefits to them. It is advisable, however, to keep a record of what money is earned, and for which jobs, if you are your child's employer, if for no other reason than to show her that you treat her employment as a commodity to be dealt with professionally and not as a hit-or-miss arrangement which can be put off, postponed, or neglected until another time. Your professionalism about the job arrangement will encourage your teen to be professional, too. If you are hiring a neighbor's child, records of payment will also enable you to show how much work and money have traded hands between you. It will also help both of you when the time comes to negotiate increases in salary or to find areas where more money might be earned in the future.

PARENTS' NEEDS VERSUS
CHILDREN'S NEEDS

When trying to determine if a part-time job is suitable for your teen, you must first be sure to separate your needs from your child's. Just because you think she has enough to keep her busy without working doesn't mean that that's necessarily the case. Maybe you don't have time to drive her to her job or be available as a backup if your teen baby-sits, for example. Perhaps you don't want to be responsible for other peoples' children or property that your child will be in contact with through her job.

Another objection may be that you think your child is already overcommitted to after-school activities. This is the so-called hurried-child syndrome, where your child has every lesson that is available and little time for anything else.

It used to be that kids had time to play, read, or just daydream, but now parents try to have their kids learn everything possible during the day and early evening too. All parents want to give their children opportunities, but what do parents get from all this? Some parents bask in their children's limelight if they perform well. Others feel that "keeping up" is what is expected in their neighborhood. There is competition to have successful children. Hurrying kids into programmed activities keeps them busy and in the running to be the prize kid on the block. But these activities don't always offer the same advantages that getting out and holding a job will.

Certainly the child's maturity level has to be taken into consideration when discussing part-time jobs, but don't underestimate your child's potential. Without trying something, a teen can never know what he's ready to do. Indeed, those parents who don't think their adolescents are reliable or mature enough to work may not want them to work because of the parents' own needs. It is through the experience of holding a job that your teen will become more reliable. Conversely, if you convey to him that he is unreliable, he will probably behave in a way to prove that you are right. When you have a positive attitude regarding your teen's reliability, he senses your desire to help him be more grown up.

Sometimes watching your children begin a work experience seems frightening—as if they are growing up and assuming adult responsibilities too soon. But every parent's goal should be to produce well-adjusted, independent children. What better way to accomplish this goal than to let your child's innate desire to be self-sufficient emerge through the work experience. This experience will be especially rewarding to the child if you have provided him with the financial facts of life.

In the case where the child's grades may not be so good, it might seem that work would interfere with studying. But it is impossible to force a child to study all the time, and it's even possible that a job could be helpful with studies, since it could build self-confidence and improve concentration. You must determine how many hours of study are necessary for the child to maintain his grades and if he would manage his time better if he had a part-time job.

Children who are having difficulty with math might benefit by doing real-life math problems, such as those required by a paper route. Record keeping, making change, adding, subtracting, and other math functions are a part of this job. Reading out loud is a good way to improve in English. A child having difficulty with a foreign language might exchange English lessons with a foreign kid his own age or younger for help with that teen's language.

Some kids will neglect their schoolwork. Educators are concerned about kids coming to school tired from working late hours, and falling asleep in class. There are laws that prohibit kids from working during school hours and limit how much they can work in the evenings and on weekends, too. Some teens will assume the attitude that if they can bring home a paycheck, they no longer need to be a student; nor do they need to be accountable to their parents. If you notice any of these signs, take action immediately. Teens still need your guidance, so if you believe that too much work is intruding on play or studying, it's time for a serious talk with your teen.

HELPING YOUR TEEN TO GET STARTED

Once the issues surrounding getting a job are resolved, it is tempting to jump in with two feet to help your child get started. Sometimes parents will even use their own networking skills to get their child a job because it seems simple and straightforward; however, the easiest way to get the child a job is not necessarily the best. Unless you know what it is that your child wants to do, there's a chance you'd come up with something unsuitable. In that case, the teen would be stuck with a job he doesn't care for and would feel that he can't quit because that would disappoint you. In addition, if he's working for a friend of the family or a relative, he may feel additional pressure which can be difficult under the best of circumstances. It's much easier to work or quit when your boss is a stranger.

The best approach is a hands-off one. Don't get a job for your child. Don't decide what kind of job he should look for, and don't take over his job in the event he can't make it for one reason or another. Instead, show interest and support. Let him know you're there if he has a question or needs you and that you support his decision, even if you don't. A healthy involvement, not interference, is your goal.

When your teen comes up with a plan of his own, you can help him envision the details necessary to make it succeed. Deanne helped her daughter make some notes before she made telephone calls to ask for part-time help. Susan wanted to sell figurines she painted, but first she had to buy supplies, figure out how many items she could make in a hurry if a store wanted them, and what she could charge. Once an idea is clear, it is ready to be pursued. Although it might be tempting to tell your child what to do, how to make telephone calls, what to say to strangers, it's better to be available as a consultant.

You can role-play with your child to help him get over the initial shyness that probably exists in approaching strangers to buy whatever product or service he's offering. Those kids who are too shy to proceed on their own might be encouraged to get a friend to work along with them. If your teen tries to sell something by telephone, most people will say they're not interested. The child can get discouraged easily as a result. What you can do at the start is alert the child to this possibility and assure him that if he keeps going and trying, he'll be able to come up with a customer. Also, the child needs to know that just because somebody says no, that doesn't mean the teen is rejected. It simply means that the other person has needs too, and what is being offered just doesn't fit in at the moment. Rejection does hurt, but it is not to be taken personally.

If your child has a definite desire to earn money but can't seem to find a way to do so, brainstorming is the best way to begin. Have your child write down all the possible ideas that pop into his mind about the kinds of jobs that may or may not be worthy of thinking about or pursuing. Just think of ideas. After getting these first thoughts down, you can point the discussion to a new direction. What are your child's special interests and hobbies which could be developed into some kind of work? What crafts does he like? Is he good with his hands? Larry could drill holes in cement walls for curtain rods and bookcases. He made money through high school and college doing this, since there was a large turnover of people in his apartment-house complex. Mark was good at carpentry, so he made up some flyers saying he could build window boxes, birdhouses, and bookshelves. Carol bought a gross of "slap bracelets" with her father's help and sold them to her classmates for a tidy profit when they were the "in" thing for showing friendship. Ask your child to think of some different things that people need done in their homes and around their property.

Think of the kinds of jobs that shopkeepers in the area could delegate. Can your child fix anything? What kind of help could your child offer to pet and plant owners? What kinds of jobs do other kids have? What did you do to earn money as a teenager? Suggest that your teen look at the bulletin board at the supermarket to see if there are any notices for extra help. If there is a local newspaper, there are want ads to look at to get more ideas. Sometimes entrepreneurs who work at home need help with mailings, filing, and odd typing jobs. Nonprofit organizations need help with these details too. Do you belong to any groups that your teen could contact? Think of community groups and church groups that might need help. Libraries hire kids after school to sort books. Some apartment houses have bulletin boards in the laundry room where your child could post a notice about his product or services.

GOALS OF AGE FOURTEEN TO FIFTEEN

- **Understand the benefits of having a job, including independence.**

- **Assess personal skills to determine a suitable job.**

- **Consider taking at-home work experiences into the neighborhood.**

- **Determine if your child's needs are being met through a job.**

- **Manage a job without it interfering with schoolwork.**

12

YOUR FIFTEEN TO SIXTEEN YEAR OLD

IT WAS VISITING DAY AT CAMP. ALL THE KIDS WERE ANXIOUSLY waiting for their parents to pull into the large parking lot by the ball field. Kevin tried to keep his attention on the softball game, but the fancy, expensive cars going past him were distracting. His family car was a three-year-old Chevy, and he felt embarrassed about that. "What kind of a car do you have?" someone asked him. Without too much hesitation, he said, "We have a BMW and a Chevrolet, but I think the BMW is in the shop."

PEER PRESSURE

By fifteen, teens like Kevin approach money as if it has a magical quality. It promises to be the means to social success. Kevin wanted to be like the rest of the kids. He hoped to belong by keeping up with them materially. Kevin's story may have been believable the first time, but if he continues to pretend, he will eventually be exposed and will lose his credibility. He's a product of the "Me Generation," fostered by a system that encourages keeping up with your neighbor. The emphasis on material objects is everywhere, from the ever-present media and its advertisers to the temptations in every store.

Behind the pressures to buy are underlying messages that respect and self-esteem are the prizes of ownership. "Things" speak louder than words. "Things 'R' Us" describes the current way we communicate and compete with others. Things are symbols of status and are extensions of ourselves. "It's me" is a common expression people use to describe a style that becomes them. Possessions serve to impress on others who we are, what we value, and what group we belong to.

Not long ago, it wasn't "nice" to be overtly materialistic. It was impolite to talk about how much money you spent. Showing off was crass and a sign of social climbing. Now, new possessions are the focus of conversations. Though blatant consumption has toned down since the 1980s, there is still constant temptation to spend money to adorn children, homes, and ourselves. There is an obvious need to be attractive and admired, even when money is in short supply. People continue to buy, but they will look for less expensive purchases.

SUBSTITUTING POSSESSIONS
FOR SELF-ESTEEM

Adolescence is characterized by self-doubt and anxiety. It is an excruciating time for teens, who want to know where and how well they can fit in comfortably. They watch themselves self-consciously as they try to dress and act as their friends do. They look to their friends for loyalty, belonging, and strength. That is why they talk on the telephone so much and why they need to dress like their friends. You may not care for their friends or how they look, but you won't have much impact on changing them. Defeating your parental control is what they want the most.

Since kids need to feel good about themselves, they usually try some external means to achieve this. Some work hard to get good grades, become athletic stars because winning gets them the recognition they crave, or wear clothing considered fashionable by the group to feel secure. Others believe they are what they own, and possessions become all-important to their self-esteem.

It is very common for teenagers to have misconceptions about what parents and others expect of them. Freddy lives in Florida in an upscale neighborhood where many people have swimming pools. He didn't have many friends, so his mother asked him why he didn't invite some classmates over to swim as a way to start a friendship or two. Freddy finally admitted he didn't want to because, "The other kids have bigger pools." If a child can believe that the size of a pool influences friendship, he is probably confused about what is important. Too often, superficial things replace solid values. If you don't ask, you won't find out what other funny ideas may keep your child from what he wants.

It may be that teenagers no longer get the opportunity to create, investigate, or try out activities that could help them feel a sense of self-worth through achievement. When any challenge is set and then met, esteem grows. The inner feeling that a child gets from *knowing* he can do something is based on positive experiences, which bring pride and a sense of success. Sometimes it's hard to take some risks that can bring rewards, so some give in to the lethargy. The skills that are basic to daily living are viewed as chores, not chances to gain a sense of competence. These days, doing well on a video game passes as personal success and effectiveness. Improving one's score substitutes for completing challenging tasks and taking personal pleasure in them.

THE PARENTAL ROLE

There are parents who want to be helpful, especially if they think their child has a social problem. Buying kids bigger and better toys works temporarily to get some attention. Older kids get cars and younger ones get Ping-Pong and pool tables, electronic gadgets, and other expensive items. However, deep down, the teen knows that it's the possession, not him, that draws people.

As soon as Angie showed an interest in horses, her mother started several part-time jobs to buy one for her. The kids at the stable were from affluent homes, and Angie's mother wanted her to befriend them. She also thought that if she worked hard and sacrificed, some day Angie would repay her. Buying the horse was a form of investment that didn't pay off, since this gift was merely one in a large pattern of indulgences. The hidden message behind this gift was not spoken out loud until Angie rejected her mother's request for help years later. When asked, "How could you treat me this way after I struggled to give you everything?" Angie's answer was, "I never asked you to struggle to buy me things."

Impressing people may also be due to the parents' need for esteem. There's so much competition for status. Kids with a successful image reflect well on their parents and can satisfy their parents' need to "keep up with the Joneses."

But as we outlined before, kids who are given things all the time don't really appreciate them. Their motivation to earn money is weakened. Their self-esteem suffers because more importance is placed on their image than on who they are underneath the clothing. Material objects wear out and need to be replaced all the time, so those who get caught up in the notion that ownership confirms self-esteem are doomed to a pattern of repeated shopping trips.

There's also stress involved in continual spending, and just as tolerance builds with alcohol and drugs, so does the ever-increasing need for higher-quality possessions to maintain a sense of self-worth.

Experiencing purchasing power is a part of growing up; teens who continue to base their self-esteem on possessions will suffer if they don't grow out of this stage. Many kids spend too much time trying to maintain their image. As a result, their personal values don't get questioned enough, nor do their relationships with others deepen. Their life seems shallow and uninvolved, so it's no wonder they are not as happy as they want to be and even become suicidal.

There's so much emphasis on paying for pleasure that kids sneer at simple and free delights. They don't value free things. They crave newness constantly, since they are so used to being stimulated by the media. There's always a new product to help you feel better in some way. Unfortunately, those kids who look to others for approval and to things for validation don't improve their self-esteem. Ultimately, it's up to parents to monitor their teen's spending sprees, whether the child has a job or not, to determine if a sense of ownership is replacing a sense of worthiness.

While teenagers struggle to compare themselves with others, it is still best for them to see how they can improve and grow within themselves, rather than for the sake of being better than or having more than somebody else. Keeping up with others for the sake of appearances is not what raises self-esteem, nor is belittling others to raise one's own status.

WHAT TO DO ABOUT
EXCESSIVE SPENDING

Despite the peer pressure and the verbal yearnings you may hear from your kids, saying no is still the best way to cut down on excessive spending. Let your child know that he doesn't need things in order to be liked. Ownership is nice, but it doesn't make kids popular or even happy in the long run. See if there's a way your teen can work for what he wants. If it's important enough to him, he will agree to earn the money.

Esther lives in Beverly Hills, the peer-pressure capital of California. "Disneyland, again?" she says is a common response from jaded kids who grew up with the most and the best of everything. Her two sons frequently attend upscale birthday parties where thousand-dollar carousels and hired bands are not unusual. Early on, she and her husband made clear to their children that they would not spend money excessively on items they didn't believe in. Esther often told them, "I am who I am. I don't apologize for not entertaining lavishly." When it came time for her oldest son's Bar Mitzvah, he concurred that a modest family luncheon was the best way to celebrate. He also came up with the idea to give some of his gift money to charity.

When her sons hit her with the line, "All the other kids are going on group dates," Esther said, "Daddy and I have a bias against group dates. We can't allow you to do something we don't feel comfortable with. I know it must be hard on you not to go out as a group, but can't you think of another way to be with your friends without hanging out at the mall?" She recommends empathizing, listening, and compromising in order to combat peer pressures.

"Life is full of choices," another parent told her teenage daughters. "If you want clothes from The Gap and Benetton, as your friends have, then you have the choice to spend your money on one or two expensive items or go for more things at less-pricey stores."

Tara also liked offering her son, Adam, choices. She was not enamored of one-hundred-and-fifty-dollar pump sneakers, but she told Adam she'd give him fifty dollars toward the sneakers of his choice. He did some comparative shopping and was eventually able to find his brand for a somewhat lower price, and he paid the difference.

No matter what socioeconomic class kids come from, there are always richer kids who have more. Even in the most affluent circles, there's an undercurrent of deprivation designed to stir up guilt in the parents who haven't "given enough" to their children. Since no one has everything, there's a lot of needless guilt out there. Kids have to learn that, even if you have an ample supply of money, there are other considerations to think about before making purchases.

Since kids copy their parents, each of us must question what message we present to our teenagers. What do you work so hard to achieve? Is it quality of life that drives you or is it the desire for a higher standard of living? If consumption is a way of life, then you may have to do some changing if you want your kids to be less competitive.

Examine your own ideas about possessions. Some people constantly redecorate, while others make do with what they have. Some have heirlooms, while others don't want the memories. Some pay less and have more, and others have fewer but better things.

The style you choose for your furnishings tells a lot about you and your values. For example, antique lovers preserve the past. Americana shows respect for what is traditional. Stainless steel and formica are practical and new. Custom furniture says you want things your way. White furnishings tell your guests to be careful.

Recall the process you went through when you bought your furniture. What was important to you? Comfort, price, look, and quality may be important, but the fantasies behind the purchases count more. Perhaps starring in your own production was a thought. Having a period theme or a color-coordinated color scheme might convey your good taste or the image of harmony in your home. Entertaining others royally may have prompted you to buy expensive china, silver, and crystal. Yet entertaining others casually can cost a lot of money too, when you figure in the expense of a gas barbeque, lawn furniture, and a gardener.

How did you decide what to buy? Were the family members asked for their suggestions? Was it a cause for celebration when the new furniture arrived or just business as usual? Did you feel a sense of satisfaction from saving and shopping for your purchases, or was it a chore? .

Your kids watch you and pick up messages. They sense your own desires to compete or keep up and may question your priorities. For example, kids who want more attention may feel neglected if financial pressures drive you to work longer hours. They don't realize that it costs more just to stay in place these days. While they may like the comforts you are able to provide, they may rebel by wanting nothing of the material world. Many embrace the counterculture that values things money can't buy. Some wear cheap clothes, don't cut their hair, don't work, hang out, and "live off the land." Others take up causes that have meaning for the betterment of society.

Some use their money to experiment with drugs and alcohol. Their underlying anxieties and insecurities seem to go away when they take these substances, and they don't have to think about grades and other pressures of school life. Chemical substances are the means for finding friends, loosening up inhibitions, and covering up uncomfortable feelings instead of learning to cope with them.

If you suspect your teen is abusing drugs, it's time to talk and to stop the allowance. This is a prime example of when it's perfectly acceptable to withhold money. When you discipline, you show you care. Some kids crave attention and will turn to substance abuse when they feel neglected at home. When they get into trouble or hurt themselves, they are actually begging for limits, since they obviously can't set limits for themselves.

Sometimes it's our teenagers who reject spending and become individuals. Marge's daughter, Nancy, chose to go to a public high school for teenagers with artistic talent, because she was unhappy with the competitive atmosphere at her private high school. Nancy was fed up with talking about shopping, expensive clothes, and big parties. She did well at the new school and made friends with people whose values were similar to hers. Nancy became so self-confident that she began to wear thrift-shop clothes and shaved her head. One evening, Nancy and her mother were walking to an Ethiopian restaurant on the Lower East Side of Manhattan, a decidedly unfancy part of town. Marge noticed that passersby looked them over from top to bottom. Marge blurted out, "I can't stand how everybody is staring at you." Nancy turned to her mother, who was in her best business suit, carrying a Gucci bag, and wearing alligator pumps, and said, "They're staring at *you* not me!" Marge needed to be more tolerant of Nancy's new image and to realize that it was probably more healthy for Nancy to be in touch with her true values than to be looking toward money and its purchasing power for self-esteem.

Have a talk with your kids about what's important to them. Listen to them without correcting or criticizing. Help them to talk about the things that are valuable inside them and others. Ask them for suggestions of what to do for fun that doesn't cost money. What are their thoughts about the kids who seem to have it all? How do you and your kids define success? What are successful people like in your teenagers' eyes?

Help your kids to guard against being sucked into keeping up with others. Let them know that what other people think is not as important as how they view themselves. Convey the attitude that it's more beneficial to improve themselves and their relationships than to compete with others. Learning to approve of yourself is cheaper, lasts longer, and is definitely more reliable than looking to others for validation. It is hoped that kids will be independent enough to make their own decisions and will say that the "Joneses" are not who they want to be. As kids experiment with their own styles, they learn what they like and what feels comfortable to them.

GOALS OF AGE FIFTEEN TO SIXTEEN

- **Resist using money as a way to boost self-esteem.**

- **Express self through meaningful activities, rather than by shopping.**

- **Achieve for personal satisfaction, not for the approval of others.**

- **Question societal pressures of materialism.**

- **Find constructive ways to cope with feelings of anxiety and insecurity.**

- **Think about what personal virtues make one a success.**

13

YOUR SIXTEEN TO SEVENTEEN YEAR OLD

LEARNING TO BE A SAVVY SHOPPER

DOROTHY GAVE HER SON, DANNY, TWO HUNDRED DOLLARS and helped him list the clothing items he was to buy. He found a wonderful fifty-dollar shirt but came home without socks and underwear. He "didn't have enough money for them" and thought Dorothy would ante up some extra cash, but she gave Danny a choice instead: Return the expensive shirt or do without socks and underwear. Danny decided to make do with his mismatched tube socks and washed-out Jockey shorts until Christmastime, when he got these essentials as a gift from his grandmother. Dorothy also was firm with her daughter, Gwen, who wanted new designer jeans. "I can't afford two pairs," she said. "You have the choice of getting one pair of designer jeans or two pairs of the regular no-name variety." Gwen chose the designer jeans that time but subsequently thought it was a better deal to have quantity rather than quality.

Sandy's father knew that when she shopped she didn't think much about the bills that would come in at the end of the month. He cured her of impulse shopping by helping her to plan ahead. They talked about what she had, what she needed, and what she would like to have. "If it doesn't work out on paper, then it won't work out in reality," he continually reminded her, so they worked out a budget as well as a wish list. Together, they planned what she could buy each month, given the amount of money she had from her allowance and her part-time job. Sandy saw that it would take a year for her to buy some expensive items she wanted, and she accepted the fact. The planning sheet helped her learn how to manage her money even after she left home.

Teens can be quite sophisticated about different kinds of stores and products. After all, they've been shopping with you for sixteen years, and they've been exposed to name brands on hundreds of shopping bags. When they go out on their own, they shop where their friends do, especially in trendy franchise shops, such as The GAP, Benetton, factory outlets, thrift shops, and army-navy supply stores. But wherever they go, they will notice that there are different prices for similar items. Teens who start to shop on their own need some tips for getting through the stores. By sixteen, they are old enough to comparison shop, read the fine print on warranties, and know their rights as consumers.

Kids need to know the meanings of *special sales, liquidation sales*, and *suggested retail price*, as well as other terms, to help them become savvy shoppers. When an item is marked down from the retail price, then it is *on sale*. When special merchandise is brought in because manufacturers could not sell it at the price that they wanted, or because it is inferior in quality, it is called *special sale*. Liquidation sales are usually for turning a large inventory into cash quickly, but some stores can go on advertising this way for years. Alert kids that *Going out of Business* signs don't necessarily mean that people are ready to vacate their premises. It can be a way to lure your teen into their store.

There can be confusion over pricing. For example, the *suggested retail price* is something most people don't pay. This is usually printed on the packaging to give the consumer an idea of what the manufacturer thinks the item could sell for, but the store can put a lower price on the product to give the effect of a bargain. Even prices that appear in dealers' catalogues may be inflated to give the dealer the chance to "discount" items. Mail-order catalogues, however, give the going price. When things are on sale at fifty-percent off, you have to know what the original price was and if it was a real price or one no one pays. If something is fifty-percent off a suggested retail price, it may not be as big a bargain as it seems.

Basically, kids need to be taught what *quality* means. Quality doesn't necessarily come in a brand name. Show kids how things are made. See if designs meet at the seams, whether buttonholes are big enough for the buttons to go through, and talk about tailoring. See if a skirt has a lining and if a coat lining is sewn in or just hangs loosely.

Just because items are made from cotton or wool doesn't necessarily mean that they are top quality. There are different grades of fabrics, and some wear well and others don't. A synthetic blend can keep clothing from wrinkling. One-hundred-percent cotton clothing may feel fine, but unless teens are willing to iron it, let them know that *synthetic* is not a four-letter word.

Your teen ought to know a store's policy. Some stores give you your money back when you return things, while others give a credit slip that can be applied to future purchases. Some will only allow you to make an even exchange. Items such as bathing suits are nonreturnable. Look for signs at the cash register which indicate that items are not refundable. If something is listed as *final sale*, it probably can't be returned or exchanged, which means the shopper better be sure that he wants the item before buying or ordering it.

WARRANTIES AND SMALL PRINT

When your teen is considering the purchase of an appliance or electronic item, she should understand what a warranty signifies. A warranty is the same as a guarantee. This is where you will find the *small print*—vital bits of information that say if the manufacturer or the store will be backing up the merchandise in the event of defects. Warranties may just cover the price of parts and not the labor involved in the repair; the labor charge can be substantial. Warranties might be something to negotiate, especially if an item is bought at a discount store which advertises that it will beat anybody's price. For example, find out if there is a loaner or a replacement you can use if your computer or typewriter is being fixed. Ask for this in writing from the dealer if you think it's important to you and the dealer wants to make a fast sale. Sometimes the first year of coverage is different from the subsequent ones if it's a five-year guarantee. A smart consumer has to be as aware as possible about the types of protection available. Encourage your child to mail in warranty cards that come with the purchase before they get lost.

As far as returning defective merchandise goes, kids this age are able to do it themselves. They need to know that they don't have to make a big fuss when they go back to the store, but they do need the receipt or sales slip as proof of purchase as well as the original packaging, so there should be a place where these items can be kept. The customer-service person or sales clerk is your teen's first person to approach with a complaint, but there's no need to shout or make threats. Most stores will accept merchandise for credit or for refund. If the sales clerk or customer-service representative isn't responsive, then it's appropriate to ask for the manager or a supervisor. If that person doesn't help, then it's fine to say in a calm voice that a complaint will be filed with the appropriate consumer agency. Get the name of the president of the company by asking for it right then and there, or call the store and ask the operator for it so your teen can write a letter of complaint. A note to the Better Business Bureau can help too.

BUYING ELECTRONICS

Teenagers are ready to spend their discretionary dollars on radios, cassette-tape players, CD players, and a myriad of other gadgets that are fun and expensive. There are so many choices of brands, options, and different types of stores that sell the same items at varying prices that kids are well advised to do some homework before they go shopping.

Encourage kids to know as much as possible about the item they want to buy before finding the store that is best suited to supplying that item. There are many magazines that advertise and analyze the latest products, and they should be read. Learn to scrutinize ads and learn model numbers as well as brand names. *Consumer Reports* are available in the library for this purpose, and Consumers Union also publishes a magazine with consumer tips for kids, *Penny Power*, which they can get through their school or by subscription.

As with other types of purchases, talking to friends is helpful. They can answer questions about what they like, don't like, and where they did their shopping if they already own an item your child wants to purchase. Determining what features are desirable and which are useless can affect the price, since pared-down models are usually cheaper. A knowledgable adult can also help educate your teen, but it should be someone your child respects and with whom he agrees to discuss his purchase.

After researching the item, the next step is to figure out where to go shopping. Some stores will quote prices over the phone, so it's important to know brand and model number if you want to begin your research this way. Department stores give good service but, unless they have a sale, usually charge more than discount stores. The selection at a department store usually covers well-known brands, whereas discount or specialty stores generally have a store brand, which might be rated higher and priced lower. Again, check your consumer publications.

The discount chains that advertise heavily and claim the lowest prices in town will actually often offer to lower their price if some other store advertises the same model and brand at a lower price. It pays to clip out competitors' ads to show to the salesperson when asking him to meet or beat the price. In such stores, the salespeople don't want to spend time negotiating, since their commissions are a percentage of the selling price. They may not be willing to educate you about the product you're interested in, but they are required to honor the lowest price as presented in the ad.

The bigger discount stores with no chain name usually have offbeat brands. They do not provide service, and that means no questions and no returns allowed. These stores have the lowest prices, but it's imperative that you know everything about the product, including the cost.

Unfortunately, not all stores have good business practices. Be wary of a few tricks. The most common one is called "bait and switch." This is done by advertising something with a very low price to get customers to come into the store. When people ask for the specially priced item, they say they're sold out and will try to sell you a more expensive item instead. Unfortunately, a teenager can be a good target for such poor salesmanship.

Another pitfall to watch for is if a product doesn't have a box, or if it looks a bit shopworn, because it may be a demonstration model. Stores want to move "demos" out of the store when new models are due to arrive. These items can be great bargains, but some stores tout them as new. Customers who ask for discounts usually get them. It can be a good idea to buy a demo, providing a warranty comes with it.

Sometimes boxed items have no prices marked on them. If you seem to have no idea what the price ought to be, the store will try to charge you what they think you'll pay. This is illegal. As always, education is your best defense.

CARS

Next to cash, kids want cars of their own. They want the freedom to come and go as they wish, and they want to do it in style. Some work hard to save the money for a used car, and others get a new car for a graduation present. If the family car is aging but not dead yet, then some teens fall heir to it when they get their driver's license and Dad and Mom shop around for a new one.

When considering a car for your teen, have a talk about the expenses and responsibilities of ownership. Decide who will pay for the car loan, insurance, gas, maintenance, repairs, and parking. Make sure your teen can afford all the hidden costs involved in owning a car. If the figures are too high when putting pen to paper, this is a good time to discuss ways for your teen to make some money.

Next to buying a house, a car is probably the most expensive item anyone purchases. Knowing how to shop for one is important, since negotiation is expected and there are numerous options to consider. As with everything else, the more informed one is the better, since dealers have been known to take advantage of unsuspecting souls. Look up information about your teen's car of choice in magazines such as *Consumer Reports, Motor Trend*, and *Car and Driver*. They are easy to find in most libraries. Get the manufacturer's invoice price, and use that as your base when you bargain. The dealer's list price, or the "sticker price," is already jacked up with extras, so it's advantageous to nail down the car's base value. This information is in books such as *Edmund's New Car Guides* and *Consumer Reports*. They are sold at bookstores. If you are a member of AAA, ask if they have information on the prices of options and if they can send you a computer printout.

If you know your budget, you won't be tempted with the extras that dealers try to sell. The "closers" are the people to be wary of, since they are the last ones you talk to before closing your deal. They may try to sell maintenance packages that you don't need. They also may be the ones to handle the financing of the car.

It's to the buyer's advantage to explore the types of financing available before going to dealers. Banks, credit unions, and thrifts have different deals. Have your teen do the research. Once becoming familiar with them, it's easier to spot a good deal if the car manufacturer offers a special loan. Compare their deal with that of factory financing through such auto-maker financial subsidiaries as General Motors Acceptance Corporation. Beware of thinking solely in terms of monthly payments. Get the whole picture with costs, interest rates, number of payments, and other terms.

Leasing has become a popular alternative to buying. It can be cheaper, so it's worth looking into. However, if your plans are to keep the car for several years, it probably wouldn't be a good deal.

USED CARS

Most teenagers will opt to buy a good used car. This can be a real challenge. These cars may sparkle on the outside, but under the hood all sorts of trouble may be lurking. You just don't know who the owner was or whether the car was taken care of properly.

As with buying a new car, research can be helpful. For a small fee, you can call *Consumer Reports* at 1–900–258–2886 and get prices on cars that go back to 1982. They can also tell you about problems they've discovered with certain models. The public library should have a copy of *The Blue Book*, a guide for used cars, published by the National Automobile Dealers Association.

There are local services that offer some diagnostic help for matters under the hood. A franchise called Auto Critic employs mechanics who will come to your used-car lot for about eighty dollars, to inspect the car you're thinking of buying. They'll put the car through as many as ninety diagnostic tests and give you a report of their findings. You can then make a more informed decision about whether to buy that particular car. If certain parts show excessive wear, make a deal with the dealer to make repairs before you buy the car.

The possibility of getting a *lemon*—a car that just doesn't operate properly—still exists, and that's why the Lemon Law was passed. You can ask your state attorney general's office to send you forms for trying to get your money back if you believe you've purchased a lemon and if the dealer gives you a hard time. The details of your breakdowns, repairs, mileage, and bills are necessary for your case. Also, to qualify, the *same* problem has to be repaired three times, and not related problems, as is more common. Try to make a deal with the dealer to refund your money or to apply your purchase price to another car. Writing a letter to the Better Business Bureau is appropriate if you're treated badly.

JOINING TAPE AND CD CLUBS

Teens want music in every conceivable way. Whether it's tapes, CD's, or records, kids listen to music as it blasts through radios, stereos, and headsets. It's an enormous business, and unless kids use their library cards to borrow albums or get gift certificates to music stores, they'll be spending a good deal of their discretionary money on music.

For kids who prefer to shop at home through catalogues, music clubs such as BMG, Columbia House, and MTV offer a viable alternative. There are pros and cons with this too, however. Joining a club seems like a wonderful deal, since they usually offer free selections as an enticement. But this offer depends on your child's promise to purchase a certain number of tapes and CD's at the regular price. The prices are lower than at some stores, but the cost of postage and handling has to be considered.

Usually, the free selections these clubs offer are popular favorites, but the subsequent choices for purchasing are not. Clubs don't offer the latest albums because the recording companies don't release them to clubs until they've sold in stores for higher prices first. While the clubs have some of the top-thirty hits, they may not be the ones your teen craves, and if your teen wants the very latest releases, it's best to shop the sales in music stores rather than join a club. It's a good idea to take a look at the catalogues of clubs before joining, at any rate.

Clubs such as Columbia House will mail selections automatically each month, unless they are told in writing not to do so. They ask

the kids to check off what they want or whether they'll pass altogether, but unless the card is mailed back on time, the club will
send their "Pick of the Month." Kids who are not too well organized can find lots of unwanted tapes and CD's in their mailbox, as
well as the bills for them.

Unwanted tapes can be returned to the company, however. If
the package is not opened, there's no charge for postage. Just write
"Refused" on the box.

The *Noteworthy Music Catalogue,* from Nashua, New Hampshire,
sells CD's without club membership. Smart shoppers who order
more than one CD at a time can get both top hits and low prices,
since the postage fee is less for bulk orders. If kids get together to
place an order, they can divide the postage and get a group bargain. This company requires a credit card for payments, so you
may have to get involved initially and then ask for reimbursement
from the kids.

NEGOTIATING PRICES

When two people come together to do business, the best of all
worlds is for each to be satisfied. In recessionary times, it's easier
to bargain for better prices, and even teens should try it.

Many business people who want to move their goods will be
amenable to selling in quantity so that the price per item is substantially reduced. If your teen is getting a school wardrobe, for
example, shop early in the summer and keep in mind that it's
possible to make a deal for such things as three T-shirts or jeans
at the price of two. Ask for a reduction by saying directly, "If I
buy three of these, how much of a discount will you give me?" or
"Since I am prepared to pay you in cash instead of by credit card,
how much will you reduce the price?" Shopkeepers have to pay
the credit-card companies from two to seven percent to handle
credit purchases, so cash ought to be worth a discount of about
that amount. If you don't like the idea of walking around with a
lot of cash, have your teen consider buying a money order at the
bank. Check with the store to make sure they will accept this,
however.

If an item is slightly soiled or damaged and it's possible to get
it cleaned or repaired, ask for a lower price. If you're prepared to
take a large package with you rather than have it delivered, say so,
and the salesperson may give a price break just because it saves

time and eliminates the extra paperwork and handling. If you know what you want and you're courageous enough to speak up and say, "I'll take this cassette player if you throw in some free blank tapes," you just might get what you want.

It's best to maintain the attitude that everything is negotiable. Prices are not carved in stone. Good deals are often made for the asking. Don't assume that salespeople will have a take-it-or-leave-it answer to your request or worry about incredulous looks or retorts such as, "Are you crazy?" If you're a serious buyer and your request isn't outlandish, why not try? But don't carry on a lengthy negotiation just for fun and then not buy the product! That just wastes everyone's time.

Some stores are better than others for bargaining. Department stores give their own discounts through sales and special purchases, but if the manager is willing, sometimes good deals are available for slightly damaged or soiled things. Talk to the owner or manager of a small store for getting the most price flexibility. Go to flea markets to practice how it's done. Try to get three items for the price of two. It's fun to do deals after a while, and confidence builds with each experience.

Some psychological tips to consider include body-language clues. If the salesperson is friendly and attentive, the chances are good that there's interest in selling to you. However, when people don't make eye contact, or if they turn away, they are conveying a lack of interest. Negative body signs include crossed arms and an insincere smile.

As a buyer, ask questions and get a demonstration so the salesperson has an investment in making a sale. Once salespeople exert time and effort, they really want to clinch the deal, even if they have to negotiate. Also, if you hesitate on the brink of a sale, that can tip the balance in your favor.

There are some things to say that can be worth money: "I love it, but it's too expensive," or "I prefer this to something I saw elsewhere, but the price at the other store was lower," or "When will this go on sale?" If you try "I'm not sure, let me give it some thought," and then return to the salesperson a couple of times with questions, that can cue the salesperson into knowing that lowering the price or including some extras might clinch the sale. "I always shop here" can also work, since stores value old customers. But be sure it's true!

GOALS OF AGE SIXTEEN TO SEVENTEEN

- Learn sales terminology and how to comparison shop.

- Learn to read warranties and understand them.

- Become an educated consumer about any major purchase as well as good business practices.

- Discuss the responsibilities, advantages, and disadvantages of music-club membership.

- Learn to negotiate for better prices, and try out your new skills.

14

YOUR SEVENTEEN TO EIGHTEEN YEAR OLD

Best-selling author Leo Buscalia tells of his experience with learning money management. Leo got an inheritance when he graduated from high school which had a stipulation connected to it: He had to use the money within six months *for fun!* Leo promptly decided to set out for Europe. Toward the end of his trip, the money was running out, so he sent a telegram to his mother, saying, "Mom. Starving. Leo." She sent him a telegram in reply, saying, "Leo. Starve. Mom." He was furious, of course, but in retrospect, he felt it was the best thing she could have done. He was forced to be resourceful and creative. The stress of not knowing where his next meal would be coming from taught him a harsh lesson. He realized quickly that if he wanted to be treated as a grown-up, he'd have to plan for his future meals and other needs. If Leo had a credit card in his wallet, he could have taken care of his emergency situation and Mom would not have known his plight—but would he have learned as much?

ESTABLISHING CREDIT

The need for credit in our present economy is so great that, without it, one can't rent a car, buy a house, or have the usual conveniences when traveling. You can't call ahead to reserve a hotel room, an airline ticket, or purchase anything over the phone.

By age seventeen, the urge for independence and freedom grows by leaps and bounds. It no longer feels right to have to ask Mom or Dad for money to go out on a date or to buy something. Kids want to break away from home, see the world, and have adult privileges. Young adults want to be grown-up and free of the restraints of parents and limited funds, so they are ripe for the not-so-subtle messages in the media to take advantage of "easy credit."

At this age, the future seems endless and so do the possibilities. This feeling of power and independence comes with the territory of growing up and moving away from home. It's a little frightening to some, but the up side is that, if your teenager feels good about herself and can handle the appropriate freedom of not accounting for her activities or expenditures as much as she used to, she is on her way to adulthood.

At seventeen, our children are nearly formed individuals who have worked hard to hone their styles. They spend money on clothing to enhance their image and their social standing. Their expenses mount, with large bills for such things as textbooks, travel, and car-insurance payments. It starts to make sense to have a credit card, especially if your teenager has proven his responsibility with money.

Additional psychological bonuses that come with establishing credit are respect and status for the teen. "Membership has its privileges," says the ad for American Express, which wants people to believe it also offers clublike advantages and social one-upmanship. The ads on television warn everyone not to leave home without it. Teens take this message seriously.

MasterCard's message of "master the possibilities" feeds into the teenage fantasy of unlimited opportunity.

The Discover Card promises adventure in its ads and titillates the wanderlust in kids who are dying to separate from home. Surely, these cards make instant gratification possible.

Michael, a student at Baruch College, applied for an American Express card when he saw that he could use their special travel-financing plan. His ticket to Paris was five hundred dollars, and he financed twenty-four installments at twenty-three dollars per month to be able to go. The card enabled him to take this trip.

While Michael's father was not thrilled about the idea of a credit card, he learned to accept it when Michael proved he could act responsibly with his monthly payments. But Michael could be the exception. Some kids give into their impulses and go wild, charging outrageous sums on their cards. Unfortunately, they find out too soon that they can't pay off their credit-card bill entirely, so they get another card to finance the first one.

Then things really can get out of control. Their self-esteem goes down and the feelings of hopelessness and desperation grow, which affects their studies and relationships, too. Of course, this is a situation which parents want to teach their teenagers to avoid.

Yes, credit has helped to raise people's standard of living and, of course, it stimulates the economy. It's convenient and has many benefits. As kids prepare to leave home, go to college, and travel, they need to know about the uses and abuses of credit. Unfortunately, the schools still do not teach this subject, so this important financial fact of life must also be passed along by parents.

What young adults need to know about credit, first of all, is that there are two different kinds of cards available: charge cards and credit cards. Some credit cards, such as those from stores, allow installment purchases with regular monthly payments and tack on interest and service fees. Visa and MasterCard will accept full payment or less and provide a minimum amount that must be paid. Charge cards, like American Express, must be paid in full when the bill is received each month.

It's a rite of passage to have a credit card. It conveys a sense of trust in the child, yet discussing appropriate purchases, and the amounts your child can charge, can feel as if you're hammering out another allowance. Indeed, you have to be clear about your own financial situation and needs while you listen to what your child has to say about his own.

It's a good idea to decide in advance how to handle large, unusual expenses. Spell out if you want your child to ask you before making a purchase or if it's okay to tell you after the fact. Discuss how this will be paid for, should the purchase be over your child's budget. Decide if you will be loaning money to your child by paying off her bills or if it will be a gift. Convey your expectation that your child will do some comparison shopping before making a major purchase. Ask your child how she feels about paying interest.

Make sure she knows that impulse purchases and everyday expenditures are areas in which it becomes easy to abuse credit. Put a cap on the amount she can charge.

Once you have covered the basics of owning a credit card, read over the initial credit contract together before signing it, in order to become familiar with consumer rights. Check out what the APR (annual percentage rate) is, since the interest adds to the cost of all items. Project how long a period it will take to pay off the "loan," should your child charge more than she can pay in any one month. Be aware of any service charges. Make sure your child knows that if the loan is not repaid, there is the distinct probability that the item purchased could be repossessed, that it still has to be paid for, and that he (or you) might get a poor credit rating in the process. Underscore the importance of spending only what money is available. Make it clear to your teen that it's best to save the money and then "borrow" from yourself, to avoid paying finance, interest, and service charges.

Today's college students are virtually bombarded by marketers who target and offer them automatic approval with their application for a credit card. Many of these students are acutely aware of the seriousness of establishing credit. This sensitivity to the importance of keeping a good track record of credit bodes well for the banks, who look for long-term customers. The banks are looking for future business while overlooking the students' low account balances and the fact that many are unemployed or paid little. Students don't need cosigners to obtain a card. A validated school ID is often the only prerequisite.

There is another way to establish credit, however, and that is to take out a personal loan and repay it. If your child has one thousand dollars or more in a savings account, he can use that amount as collateral for a loan from that bank. He won't be able to withdraw the borrowed amount from the savings account, and he'll have to come up with monthly repayments of the loan. It is hoped that he can show the bank how credit-worthy he is by repaying the loan in a prompt fashion for six months or more. He can then pay off the balance of the loan in a lump sum to avoid extra interest charges, if the bank allows this practice. The teen who establishes credit in this way will probably also be offered a credit card through the bank that made the personal loan or through another lending institution looking for new customers.

AVOIDING CREDIT CRISES

People who charge more on their cards than they can pay for at the end of each month have to pay interest charges from thirteen to twenty percent, and the companies who offer the cards don't mind a bit if you pay only the minimum amount. The card companies make their money from interest on these installment payments, and since the cost of money to banks now is only between three and four percent, you can see that the card companies are making ten to sixteen percent off of the unpaid balance on your card.

While only paying the minimum payments on your bill may seem enticing, in the long run it can be extremely costly. Lisa owes four thousand dollars on her credit card, which has a nineteen-percent interest rate. If she pays only the minimum amount, which is three percent of what she owes, or about one hundred and seventy dollars a month, she'll end up paying $3,900 in interest thirteen years down the road. She would pay just about double for each item she bought. One only has to think of Lisa to understand how important it is to teach kids about the proper use of credit. If your charge balance is paid in full, the banks don't make a profit from you unless you pay an annual fee for the use of the card.

People who default or make late payments are often termed "deadbeats" or "jugglers" by lending institutions. It's this group that causes banks to charge higher fees. Unfortunately, the banks don't know who will be a good subsidizing customer for their services and who will become a deadbeat. While having a job or a history of paying off a loan are good indicators that the customer is credit-worthy, they're not guarantees. Banks send out many invitations to "preferred customers" to take advantage of a preapproved credit line and sign up for a new card. This makes the customer feel special and rewarded; however, it might also seduce him into debt.

The credit line banks offer is a short-term loan, but it has the allure of being "extra money." It is a universal truth that everybody, no matter how wealthy, wants and could use extra money. There is always something more to buy, to improve, to replace, and to enjoy. Shopping is still the favorite American pastime. The fantasy of having extra money is powerful. Add that to the illusion that a plastic card is not real money, and you get people who deny that they have to pay with real money at the end of the month.

A good credit history is important, and this is the message you should impress upon your teenager. Students who have credit cards need to know their financial limits, or they can quickly fall into the deadbeat or juggler group. If they can't afford to make their interest payments, they risk losing their valuable credit rating.

Kids need to know that, without a good credit history, they risk losing the trust which stores and banks have in them. If that happens, their credit rating goes down and they're called a poor credit risk. When they use credit, they must know that they are promising to pay off their debt on time. Credit bureaus keep a record of whether they pay on time and how much they pay. The quicker the bills are paid, the better.

A good credit history will make borrowing money for such things as a car or a house easier. It will be a good reference if your child applies for a job or wants to rent an apartment.

The agency that keeps the credit-history file is a credit bureau. The biggest ones are Equifax, TRW, and Trans Union. They have information on one hundred and fifty million Americans. From time to time, it's a good idea to pay a small fee, if necessary, and request your own credit report to make sure it's correct. The telephone book lists these agencies under "Credit Bureaus." You can ask your creditors which bureaus they belong to.

Parents who provide their child with a credit card hope that their child will use it responsibly. If you do not talk about credit limits, proper usage, and reimbursement, you will only have another bill to pay and not a responsible teenager. This can erode the parent/child relationship and create more dependence than independence. It can be "the tie that binds." The teenager's behavior implies, "I'm still a kid and not ready for maturity." For young adults who are naturally rebellious, overusing the little plastic card is a way to communicate a revengeful "you'll pay" to their parents. Whether you are perceived by your teen as doing too much, too little, or something in between, abusing credit can be his way of saying, "I'll get you with this bill."

Wise parents will take an active role to discuss the meaning of the behavior and try to solve the problems without using money as the medium. If your child has had experience learning how to manage cash, this will be a snap. However, if your child repeatedly runs short on his allowance, borrows from friends, or asks for advances, it's not recommended that he have a credit card until he's pulled himself out of these financial pickles.

When there are too many bills and too much anxiety, there is a problem in the works, and its resolution depends on facing the factors squarely. If keeping up with the Joneses is your teen's problem, more realistic spending habits need to be examined. If holiday shopping was the cause, use cash next year to avoid "spending" the whole year paying for purchases. When binging and splurging are to blame, try to get your teen to do things to reward himself that don't cost money. If spending is a type of therapy for your teen, you should consider psychotherapy, which is cheaper and more enduring. Should your teen be purchasing items which are simply too expensive, then his desires have to be tamed and money has to be saved for these items. Credit cards were designed for convenience, not for instant wish fulfillment.

Author Judith Briles has three children: Shelley, Sheryl, and Frank. She mentions in her book, *The Dollars and Sense of Divorce*, that when they were teenagers, she put each of her children's names on one of her MasterCard accounts. Judith's wish was to teach the kids their rights and responsibilities with credit. She wanted to help her children establish their own credit files, so she added their names and Social Security numbers to the account. She also wanted them to get used to managing their own money. The understanding was that the children were to pay for what they charged. She told them her motto was, "Those who play have got to pay." There were at least a couple of times when she had to make the payments for Sheryl because she went beyond the limit she could handle. As a consequence, Judith suspended her card.

Since Shelley had been fiscally responsible, her credit report was excellent, and she began to get applications for her own Visa card when she got to be eighteen. Sheryl took longer to bring her spending habit under control, but she eventually did.

Frank took the longest route to achieving credit under his own name because he paid cash, never used his charge card, and therefore no credit bureau knew of him. He was only able to establish credit after he repaid a loan for a motorcycle. He didn't know that Judith co-signed for this loan, so he worked hard to make the payments out of fear that he'd lose the motorcycle if he missed a monthly payment.

Judith had to guarantee the loan balances until the girls turned eighteen. At that time, their payments came out of their own checking or savings accounts. Sheryl, predictably, had trouble balancing her checkbook. In fact, Judith says that she made such a wreck of the checkbook that she had to close two different accounts and start fresh to try to keep things straight. Judith secretly worried about Sheryl a lot, but when she did balance her checkbook, it was cause for celebration. If you also are on the brink of losing hope that financial management can be a reality for your child, be patient and remember that Sheryl now is a young mother who is putting money away for her son's education, and she also funds her own IRA and money-market account.

AUTOMATIC TELLER MACHINES (ATMS) AND CHECK-GUARANTEE CARDS

There are money machines on or around every corner, from which cash—in twenty-dollar bills—may be drawn. Banks have invested over five billion dollars to make banking easier for everyone. No doubt, the transaction fees for using the machines will help to recoup some of that investment. Once your child opens a checking account, a money-machine card will surely follow.

This easy access to cash has its advantages. Most young people claim that there is a feeling of independence and even power in having their money available everywhere at any time.

Angela was glad that she had an ATM card that gave her access to her money from banks out of her state. She was on the way home from a weekend away at a friend's home when she got a flat tire. She used her available cash to tip the guy who changed the tire on the highway, and she stopped at a bank in a strange town to withdraw some extra cash in case something else unforeseen happened.

People who don't keep close tabs on their spending swear by these machines, since they get their available balance on their receipts. There are some people who withdraw a set amount of cash every day or week and feel this helps them stay within their budget. They say they feel more in control of their finances when they use the machines to give them an "allowance."

While it may help some, it hurts others. There is a magical quality to getting money from a hole in the wall. Gary said, "When I get ATM money, it feels like I've won it. There's a gamelike quality to the ritual. Punch in your secret code, make a selection, and get your prize—crisp new bills. It's almost like getting a gift, except that I have to remember that I'm the giver."

Some teens overdo these transactions by taking out too much money too soon. Richard feels out of control of his finances because he "can't pass an ATM machine without collecting some 'Go' money." He says he pays for this addiction by having over one hundred dollars in transaction fees a year.

When the machines work, they can be a great convenience, but as with anything else connected to money management, they need to be used with moderation. It can help to clip an index card to the bank card to keep track of deposits and withdrawals. Explain to your teenager that machines are to be used occasionally, instead of for frequent allowances. This reduces fees and encourages planning ahead. Also, set a limit for your teen on how much money can be withdrawn in a week or a month.

Many people forget to make note of their transactions when they don't carry their checkbook with them. It's important to keep track of and to file the receipts.

Even machines make mistakes. Sometimes the deposits don't get properly credited. Since money-machine deposits aren't stamped, they aren't considered to be as legitimate as a teller's deposit slip. At the end of the month, compare them with the monthly bank statement to make sure the records are correct. If not, call the bank right away.

There is also such a thing as a check-guarantee card. Banks offer them as an all-purpose bank card that will guarantee checks up to two hundred and fifty dollars and allow ATM usage. The check-guarantee card even works as a purchase card in some stores. As your child uses the card, the amounts charged get deducted from his bank account. The bank stands ready to make advances and charge interest if there isn't enough money in the account. Your child will learn that extra charges can be avoided if he saves his money before spending it. When you and your child go to the bank to apply for this card, be sure the banker gives all the details to your child. After all, he'll be the customer, not you. Your child must remember to jot down in his checkbook how much he spends, since the money will be withdrawn from his account. Go over the monthly bank statement together to make sure there are no mistakes.

GOALS OF AGE SEVENTEEN TO EIGHTEEN

- **Recognize the need for credit and how to use it responsibly.**

- **Establish credit.**

- **Learn what is meant by credit history, collateral, finance charges, service charges, APR, and installment credit.**

- **Open a checking account and learn to balance the checkbook.**

- **Use money machines and check-guarantee cards with moderation, and keep track of transactions.**

Part Three

PROBLEMS WITH MONEY

15

COMPULSIVE SHOPPING

WHEN TOM WAS TEN, HE REGULARLY TOOK MONEY FROM HIS mother's wallet to buy candy and other gifts for friends. "It was important to me to have something I wasn't allowed to have, because I grew up in a dysfunctional family where it didn't seem to matter whether I was there or not. I felt put down and unloved. As a result, I always tried to please other people so I could get affection. I'd buy stuff for other kids so they'd be my friends."

"My Mom and I love to go shopping together," said Debby, who admitted she had at least twelve pairs of shoes and a weakness for pretty underwear, some of which still have the tags on them. "Mom and I get a 'high' from a whiff of perfume at the cosmetics counter, and we have the greatest time pulling outfits together before school starts. I always feel like I'm the best-dressed student, and I never have to pay a dime. It's like being a princess."

"My Mom gives me her credit card and sends me on my way," said Trudy. "She's too busy to shop with me, since she works full time. I don't really feel I spend too much, since Mom can afford it, but if I buy something extra like a blazer or a silk blouse that just begs to be bought, my Mom goes nuts. She cares more about that than anything else, it seems."

The teens in the preceding examples may be on the brink of becoming compulsive shoppers. Shopping satisfies their inner needs. For those who feel deprived, frustrated, bored, or depressed, shopping is a form of therapy, a quick fix to make up for uncomfortable feelings. Adults and kids temporarily feel better when they hear, "May I help you?" from some smiling, warm-hearted salesperson, whose job it is to gratify and satisfy whims and wants. It's nice to have attention from someone who seems to care and who will assure you that you look your best.

SHOPPING AS THERAPY

Shopping is stimulation to people who feel bored. "It's something to do and is usually pleasant. Everything is new all at once in the stores, and it feels good to touch or try on whatever I want," said Nicole as she went on to compare stores to casinos. "There are no windows or clocks around. I lose touch with time. I usually am among the last to leave the stores, since I don't want to miss seeing all the new merchandise. I really get away from it all when I shop."

All teenagers complain of boredom, and shopping is an accessible way to have something to do. It gives them a sense of accomplishment to buy things, and it focuses their unstructured time.

Shopping is a family experience, and kids learn to love it since it's a part of their life from birth. Kids see that they get things from stores without too much time or effort on their part. They get treats along the way and are even entertained. Shopping becomes a form of fun.

The malls have become the community centers of the suburbs, where kids hang out to socialize and show off their latest acquisitions. Some have enough belongings that their rooms resemble stores. Window shopping can't compare to being a part of the mall experience, where open-faced stores welcome wanderers who look for the newest, the latest, and the greatest goods.

What other experiences can provide such enjoyment, escape, and psychic rewards? There's even a magical quality to going shopping. Self-improvement becomes possible instantly with a new outfit. It's possible to get a new look, as well, with cosmetics. The wardrobe can reflect fantasies of romance, travel, and the exotic. You can star in your own production. Also, mothers who take their daughters on regular shopping excursions engage in a pleasant ritual where eating and talking are additional satisfactions.

Splurges and shopping sprees, however, don't necessarily indicate there's a problem with compulsive spending. Everyone from time to time gets in the mood to refresh wardrobes or rooms at home. Certainly spending is encouraged in our society, since it keeps the economy going and people employed. It's so socially acceptable that until fairly recently the problem of compulsive shopping went unnoticed. Alcoholism and compulsive eating show physical telltale signs, but being in debt doesn't.

The word *compulsive* indicates a have-to quality to this behavior. They think, "Oh, what pretty colors. I want both the magenta and the lime green." They don't think of cost as much as they think of having what catches their eye. They'd like to feel in control of their life, but the irony is that their behavior and often their bank balance are quite out of control. Compulsive shoppers usually have bulging closets and drawers, and things stashed under beds as a result of their binges. They don't know exactly what they have, but they're sure they need whatever is there to help them feel comforted and secure. Teens' overstuffed rooms may be in direct proportion to the amount of inner emptiness they feel. Symbolically, the whole act of filling up shopping bags reflects their wish to feel more complete and fulfilled.

Teens normally have the challenge of finding their identity, and they do it with clothing and through music and personal style, but those children who utilize shopping as a means of expressing themselves are trying to feel more whole, more adequate, and more attractive. Consequently, the relentless search for possessions is their attempt to impress others or to make up for some feelings of deprivation. This inner emptiness can also cause kids to turn to drugs, alcohol, food, and sex, too.

Teens who are compulsive shoppers are often insecure and constantly look to others for approval. When they get compliments, they experience them as a form of love. Their wish to please makes them pleasant to be with, since they tend to be friendly and outgoing. As a result, they get positive responses from others, which also feels like love. In their family environment, there has been some blow to their sense of self, which made them feel they weren't good, pretty, or lovable enough. Attempts to be attractive and desirable take on a desperate quality as they unconsciously hope that new clothes, accessories, and jewelry will get them the affirmation they need so badly.

For the compulsive shopper, credit cards add an element of magic and unreality to shopping. Without using cash, these people don't experience the sense of paying for their purchases. Money becomes a limitless commodity that can soothe and salve. Credit cards help the shopper deny the fact that payment is even expected. There is a temporary suspension of all sense of responsibility. The impulsive purchase can be used right away, while the bill for it hasn't even been printed.

These shopaholics rationalize their purchases by saying, "I need a little something for myself." The reasons for feeling deserving might also be due to having a hard day, being slighted or insulted, or not getting something they wanted. It could be that the weather was bad or that something else was totally out of their control.

Adolescents who cannot stop themselves from shopping get an overpowering urge to buy things they want when they may not have any need or even desire for them. They say they feel "frantic and impulsive," things seem "irresistible," and they're "out of control." Having a credit card makes these impulse-buying sprees easy.

The shopping spree is an attempt to control and remedy the inner problems of emptiness and depression. Buying new things can be a quick fix to give the impression that all is well. This temporary solution to the chronic problem of how to raise self-esteem is usually followed by a crash of feelings, where guilt, anxiety, and shame are common. Tension builds and—again—relief comes only from spending money. Since the person feels the need to repeat the behavior over and over, it is regarded as seriously as other compulsive behaviors, such as overeating, drinking, and gambling.

Many adolescents who shop too much also overeat. For them, binges may be triggered by emotions they don't want to recognize. In their history, they may have been given things, as well as food, as a substitute for real nurturance and care. Many were given whatever they asked for by well-meaning parents who wanted their kids to have everything they never had. Over time, these kids learn to use shopping as a way to feel that their parents still care for them. Many, on the other hand, would rather shop than eat, and they spend all their lunch money on clothes.

Kids also spend money to seek revenge against parents who aren't emotionally giving. These teens are starving for recognition, approval, and confirmation. Underneath, they worry that they're not lovable or good enough; otherwise, their parents would surely provide them with more guidance and love. As a result, these teens constantly seek approval from others as a way to feel okay about themselves. They will even steal to get money to buy gifts for friends.

PARENTAL INFLUENCES

Parents who constantly work or who are too self-involved may unwittingly give kids the message that love comes in packages from a store. Parents who travel a lot will "pick up something" after a business trip, even if the gift isn't of interest to the child. This way of expressing love can be passed down through the generations.

Often, expressing love is difficult. Demonstrativeness is not tasteful in some cultures or in some families. Many people are personally limited and just cannot or simply don't know how to show their feelings, while others keep their feelings to themselves out of fear that they will be misunderstood or, worse yet, not have their affection returned.

In homes where divorce, neglect of some sort, or abuse occurs, some parents attempt to assuage their guilt by buying kids things. They hope to make up for arguments or shortcomings, so they compensate, or pay off, their children with possessions. These parents often just pass out cash, since it's easier than searching for an appropriate present. Over time, children begin to equate gifts with love.

There can also be a connection between clutter and love in homes where there is a substitute of money for love. It becomes difficult for people from these families to get rid of possessions because of the emotional value placed on them.

All parents who are interested in teaching the financial facts of life should be aware of the way they influence their child's spending habits. Placing more value on money or appearances than on inner needs and emotions will not convince a child, especially in the teenage years, that she is loved for herself. It may become necessary to evaluate your own spending habits as well as your parenting skills if you suspect compulsive shopping in your child and, as with all compulsive behaviors, undertake the necessary steps to correct the situation.

WHAT TO DO

A cure for compulsive shopping can only begin if and when the shopper admits there is a problem. The financial as well as emotional areas need to be addressed by talking about the problem and putting words to the feelings in order to eliminate acting them out. This is easier said than done.

Denial of the problem can be the single most difficult roadblock to overcome. What is evident to family and friends usually gets brushed off by shopaholics. They'll say, "I don't shop a lot, so I'm not a compulsive spender," or "I'm not in debt, so I don't have a problem," or "Shopping is fun, why should I stop?"

Yes, there is a thin line between regular and compulsive spending. If you are unsure if your child has crossed that line, consider the following clues: Are your child's drawers or closet filled with things that never get worn and still have the price tags on them? Does your child buy things he doesn't need or even want? Is your child preoccupied with money and does he frequently ask for more? Does he know the prices of all sorts of odd things? Does she spend everything she gets or earns? Does she make a habit of paying for others, or lending money, as a way to make friends?

Any of this behavior is worthy of discussion, but if you see two or more symptoms, it's time to talk things over and consider that your child could be a compulsive shopper. Since kids are not in touch with the underlying reasons for shopping, and they can find it too difficult to talk about their feelings, you can share your own observations, reactions, and feelings to gently get the process going. Avoid confrontation or placing blame, since that ends discussions before they begin. Certainly, you can be empathic about wanting to have nice things and wanting to belong. Eventually, you can learn what goes on in your child's mind to trigger a shopping spree. Once you know the types of triggers, you can talk about better ways to cope.

Kids can't buy self-esteem in a store. They will feel better about themselves if they become more aware of the small, medium, and large things they do daily that make them proud. If they can learn to pat themselves on the back, they'll quit looking for others to do it for them. Helping teens reward themselves with kind words, instead of possessions, can help, too. Generally, teens are self-critical, self-doubting, and self-centered, so their efforts to be kinder to themselves and more accepting are your goal. Letting them know that you *do* care about them and want to help may be the best steps to take.

Shopping, unlike alcohol and drugs, cannot be stopped entirely. What's important is to learn how to spend in a more normal way. Facing one's bills to see how much is spent is a good dose of reality, as is taking an inventory of the closet. Carrying cash, and only the amount that is budgeted for the day, is a good idea. Knowing what you want to buy can prevent wandering around aimlessly in the store. Going only to the store or department that has what you're looking for also helps to prevent impulse purchases, as does leaving the store after one hour. Credit cards are to be handled as "controlled substances." Cut them up or lock them up. Help your child make a wish list and buy things according to a plan. Planning for a great birthday gift instead of spending money on unnecessary items can make the wait worthwhile.

PARENTAL GUIDELINES FOR DEALING WITH COMPULSIVE SHOPPING

- **Admit that there's a problem.**

- **Recognize how the problem manifests itself.**

- **Identify missing needs and put them into words.**

- **Determine what triggers buying sprees.**

- **Regain control by finding better ways to deal with feelings.**

- **Nurture the self with kind words, involvement in new activities, physical activity, and other *free* experiences.**

- **Plan ahead for shopping expenditures.**

16

SHOPLIFTING

"MY HEART POUNDS AND MY HANDS GET WET. I FEEL LIKE EV-erybody can see me, but I don't dare turn to see if anyone's really looking. I keep saying to myself, 'Take it easy, look calm,' but that's hard to do. As I walk around the store, I look for things I want. Usually, I end up at the jewelry department since I like earrings. When I find a pair I like, I just push them off the counter into my shopping bag and try on another pair to look casual. Then I leave, sweating like crazy," said Mary as she recounted her recent shoplifting experience. Although Mary hasn't yet been caught shoplifting, she is endangering herself every time she steals.

IDENTIFYING THE PROBLEM

It's hard to estimate how much money is lost by business an-nually because of shoplifting. It's more than is lost from bank robberies and could be as high as twenty-five billion dollars a year, according to the National Retail Merchants Association. More than five cents of every dollar spent goes to pay for lost or stolen merchandise, for which other consumers have to pay. A family of four, therefore, could be paying as much as twelve hundred dollars a year to make up for shoplifting.

There is also an enormous amount of money spent on security guards, convex mirrors, inventory tags, signs, detectors, and wired mannequins. Theft is a significant reason why many small businesses fail.

There are plenty of arrests, but when you consider that shoplifters steal many times before they get caught, you get a flavor of the magnitude of this problem. While many teenagers shoplift many times, some do it only once or twice and stop because they can't tolerate the guilt and anxiety associated with it. The more times they steal, the higher the likelihood is of getting caught. Teenagers are the largest group of shoplifters. Both boys and girls indulge in shoplifting.

Teens today often complain of boredom because they don't know how to entertain themselves. Television and video games have relieved children of having to invent their own creative games and play. Many children grow up learning advertising jingles instead of nursery rhymes. Add this to homes where money and love are confused, and teens turn to stealing as a way to provide "things" which, to them, mean love. The excitement of stealing relieves boredom.

When the ringleader of a group suggests lifting things for fun and excitement, it's a good bet that the other kids will follow. They feel strength in numbers, and that is why group membership is so important. They will do almost anything to show that they belong. Rich and poor kids get their kicks, as well as portions of their wardrobe, this way.

Not all kids shoplift for thrills, acceptance, or rebellion. There are many who do it because they want to have things they can't afford. There are kids who steal things for their family, and others who do it simply because they want what everybody else has. These kids see ads on television and experience well-stocked stores. They see how others who have money look, and they want to be included in the group that has nice things too. Without education, supportive families, role models, and opportunity, many do so with little or no guilt.

Some of the emotional goodies teens feel they deserve may be appreciation, care, approval, gratitude, attention, and acceptance. If they're not getting these goodies, they feel justified in stealing goods from the local stores.

It takes a child four to six years to learn the difference between right and wrong, since no one is born with a conscience and there is no such thing as an instinct called guilt. Babies know only pleasure and pain. As they grow, they give up some pleasures for the reward of getting parental approval.

Through consistent loving and supervision, parents teach kids to tell the truth, to control angry feelings, and to respect others' property. The child learns over time what will be punished and what won't. He learns from repeated experiences that his own immediate pleasure sometimes brings him pain. Eventually, he hears an inner voice repeating that of his parents: "Don't do that. That doesn't belong to you. Give that back."

Inconsistency is confusing to the child. If one parent is firm and the other winks at the child's behavior, there won't be a clear enough message about what is unacceptable. His later behavior will reflect this.

Children need to hear a warning or punishing voice and need to feel love in order for a conscience to develop. Unfortunately, many children grow up without either. Many children are punished but won't change their behavior. Presumably, this is because the children don't love the parents enough to want to be good.

Delinquent behavior in teenage years may be a by-product of circumstances in the child's early life. For example, was mother able and willing to care for the child properly or was baby left to her own devices? Too much freedom and not enough limits convey that it's all right for her to do as she pleases, and the child won't learn about respecting others' possessions.

Too much indulgence, in the form of giving the child everything she wants, may cause the child to resist growing up. She'll want to continue having what she wants, resulting in impulsive and self-centered behavior. The child doesn't learn to delay gratification or to endure some pain or tension. In later years, the child seeks ways to provide instant gratification for herself, and one way to get something when she wants it is to shoplift.

Unfortunately, there's a climate in the country that somehow looks the other way with regard to stealing. When compared to so many horrific crimes that are committed, shoplifting seems to be regarded as a minor one. Even though there's an element of shame to it, the general feeling persists that everyone does it at one time or another. One in ten shoppers is estimated to have stolen something at least once, and this usually happens when they are teenagers.

When a person is contemplating a theft, the moral teachings about stealing get superseded mentally by a prevalent, immediate need that must be met. The thought, "Don't do it," gets overwhelmed by, "Go ahead, you can do it, you deserve it." The teen acts on impulse and doesn't process the thought thoroughly. He suspends the part of his mind that might warn him against the act. It's as if another person were doing the stealing.

At the point of taking something, there may be fleeting thoughts, such as, "What am I doing? Put it back before you get caught." However, those thoughts are quickly replaced by the ones that say, "I do want this. I'm more likely to get caught if I put it back."

Some kids swear they'll never steal again because they feel so guilt-ridden. Yet, the urge to steal again can overpower them. Then, the more they shoplift, the less they think of it as right or wrong; and if a friend is included, they feel courage and treat it as a game. Shoplifters feel less responsibility when they know someone else is doing the same thing.

While parents may not actually commit punishable crimes, they may unwittingly create an atmosphere in the home where kids get the message that "everybody does this." Let's not forget that there are numerous examples of adults who steal. The news is full of stories of embezzlement, tax fraud, insider trading, bribery, and corruption. Adults take items from work and hotels all the time. Parking tickets get fixed. Kids get into the movies and on buses for half price when they shouldn't. When kids see towels from hotel chains and yellow pads taken from the office, they can get the idea that it's all right for them to steal too. They assume that anyone can take things as long as they don't get caught. Parents may teach kids not to steal from individual people, but corporations or even our government at tax time appear to be exceptions to the rules.

RATIONALIZATIONS AND REASONS

Rationalizations abound as excuses for shoplifting. Beyond wanting something for free, shoplifters typically give these reasons: "Nobody gets hurt." "Everybody knows that clothing is priced

outrageously high." "Nobody will miss this." "The store over-
charges." "Everybody gets away with it, so why can't I?"

Shoplifting satisfies some pressing inner needs for repeated offenders. It could indicate that there are problems at school, at
home, or with friends. Generally, it is the need for love that un-
derlies the behavior. This neediness has to do with feeling deserving but lacking the confirmation from others. Other reasons may
be rebellion, peer pressure, temptation, wanting something for
free, having no money, or simply the excitement of trying to get
away with illegal behavior. Some "lift" in order to get money for
drugs. It is most usually a form of compensation for feeling deprived of recognition, appreciation, and worthiness. When they
run down emotionally to "empty," they "refill" by thinking, "If I
don't get what I need, I'll steal it."

Shoplifting can be a form of rebellion and a means of separating
from parents whose rules become too stifling to live with. Parents
who go by the book will surely be upset to find their child shoplifting. Some adolescents want to upset their parents, and what better
way to do this than by snubbing one's nose at the family's values?

Some of the things kids steal have symbolic value. For example,
the stolen item could be identical to one owned by someone who
the adolescent admires. Sexy items like lingerie in some way shore
up a flagging self-concept. If a teen worries about his appearance,
he will lift items that can improve it, usually clothes. Some will
steal anything they feel they deserve, to make up for unhappy conditions at school or home.

Depression can be a major factor in shoplifting. Kids get depressed to avoid the feelings of anger, frustration, and emptiness
which they can't handle or express. Depression pushes all other
feelings away, so the excitement that shoplifting offers is a way to
feel alive at least temporarily. There is a thrill about doing something taboo in public, and that thrill accelerates the heartbeat.
Rather than talking about what is bothering them, kids often must
act out their conflicts to get rid of them.

What about stealing from friends? Is that different from stealing
from a store? It's probable that the child wants to have a souvenir
that symbolizes the good feelings of the friendship. It is a primitive
way of holding onto some crumbs of love. These kids are extremely needy. No one can really give them all that they want.
Most people would find it impossible to be on the infantile, sym-
biotic wavelength that these people crave. Rejection is the usual

result, since it's too hard to be friends with these people. This can set the child off again to salve, rather than to solve, problems through shoplifting.

KLEPTOMANIA

Shoplifting is different from kleptomania in that it is done in an occasional or experimental way, not in a compulsive, *have-to* way. If it happens on a regular basis, then kleptomania may be the problem. Also, the motivation behind the stealing can differentiate between shoplifting and kleptomania. An item lifted because the person *wants* it is different from *needing* it. There is usually no symbolic value to the item, and the person most usually can afford to pay for it. Kleptomaniacs repeatedly take things that have specific significance to them. They take what they need rather than lifting something just because nobody is looking. The shoplifter does not want to divulge how needy she is, so she takes something she wants but doesn't necessarily need.

WHAT TO DO

If a chronic shoplifter goes into therapy, there's hope of putting words to the symbolic act. It's hard for these people to set aside their impulsivity and give the ego a chance to get to work on their problem. Therapists try to build up the ego so it can have the strength to mediate between the other forces the next time the mood comes on. In the therapy process, the patient will eventually come to understand that it's love he wants. Once the patient is aware of this, the next step is to figure out how to get it without stealing things. Figuring out what can be done within one's control and without breaking the law are the goals.

Self-esteem, self-love, is the key. If you love yourself sufficiently, there's no need to look to others for approval or a pat on the back, because you can give it to yourself. You can nurture yourself better than anybody else can because you know what you want. You can be proud of yourself without waiting for parents, the boss, or others to give you the stamp of approval. Little by little, the chronic shoplifters can become more aware of what the feelings and urges are inside him. The ability to slow down and apply a little reason and judgment grows in the process. The need to defend oneself with rationalizations and denial decreases. It helps to talk to oneself instead of automatically running to stores when upsetting feelings surface. Exploring problems and finding solutions and alternatives helps to regain a sense of control.

The cure comes in the motivation to get rid of pain. When a teenager is caught and is faced with a choice of psychotherapy or jail, this may be sufficient for him to get started on stopping the problem behavior. Once the words are put to what the symbolic act is, the person can find cheaper and better alternatives to get what he or she really needs.

Teens can learn that it's too late, or impossible, to get "the goodies" from parents, and it is time to give them to themselves. Too frequently they look for approval from others, when they can give it to themselves. They can learn to recognize the small, medium, and large things they do every day to improve their own self-love. When they have learned that, there is no need to steal.

Many stores are quick to call the police and maintain a tough position, since letting kids off with just a warning can signal that the store is an easy target for future hits. If kids are caught red-handed, they will experience humiliation and embarrassment, especially if their friends see them get handcuffed and led out of the store. The younger offenders go to juvenile court, where they may be sentenced to a correctional facility, community service, or ordered to pay damages. Since shoplifters don't believe they're hurting anyone, just anonymous companies, some are ordered to pay restitution to a shopkeeper up to ten times the amount that was stolen. Shoplifting is a crime, so after age eighteen, a conviction remains a record for life.

When kids are very little and they "borrow" something, claim it as "mine," proclaim, "I need it," or say, "look what someone gave me," it doesn't mean that they have a serious problem. It signals the time to teach kids the difference between *mine* and *thine*. It takes years for the message to sink in, since, initially, the child doesn't know that money is valuable and has no idea of what personal property is.

Early punishment is the best prevention. Let the child know it's bad to pick up loose change from your dresser. Let your feelings be known that you do not approve of his taking things that don't belong to him. If your child has something that was not paid for, go with the child right away to return the item, and have the child make an apology to the shopkeeper. If the child gets a reprimand from him, that's better than hearing, "It's okay." If the child feels guilt, that is good and necessary. It might help to have the child do some extra chore so he'll have some punishment to ease the guilt. If the child cannot make immediate restitution, make sure he pays you back as soon as possible. In any event, all stolen items should be returned, and remember that it doesn't help the child if you overlook or minimize the experience. Try not to leave young children unsupervised in stores, since they may find it very tempting to lift things.

When you know your toddler took a toy from a friend, help him to know that he can't have it just because he likes playing with it. You can say to a small child, "I see that you have your friend's toy. Your friend probably wonders where it is, so you'll have to return it."

Older children need to be told that stores are not impersonal places. Help them know that real people suffer if things are not paid for: The store owner, the clerks, or other shoppers have to make up for stolen merchandise.

Giving more attention to teens is giving them what they really want. Let them know you care about them by talking, listening, and asking them questions. Find out if they need more money or what their ideas are about how to earn more. Let them know that stores are tough on shoplifters. Keep a diplomatic eye on how much money the child has and how it's spent. If you know your child's belongings, and something unfamiliar shows up, you have a right to ask to see the receipt.

PARENTAL GUIDELINES FOR DEALING WITH SHOPLIFTING

- **Talk about shoplifting in general and convey your attitude toward it.**

- **Create an atmosphere at home that does not condone white-collar crime.**

- **Insist that your child return all stolen items.**

- **Ask about problems at school or with friends if you suspect shoplifting.**

- **Help your child get what he wants without having to steal.**

17

EXCESSIVE
FRUGALITY

"My daughter still has her allowance at the end of the week. She holds on to her money so long that I wonder whether she has no expenses or she has a problem."

UNDERSTANDING PENNY
PINCHERS

Holding on to money can be a problem. Kids miss out on opportunities to go places and to socialize. Also, frugal people reduce the pleasures of the process of spending: planning, selecting, wearing, and sharing don't really excite them. *Tightwads*, whether adolescent or adult, are sometimes difficult to be around too, since they engender a sense of guilt in others. Ordinary spending can feel like squandering to people who are excessively frugal, and their spontaneity and curiosity get squelched too.

While tightwads may seem to be devoid of enjoyment, they get pleasure from saving, counting, and accumulating money. The sense of security in knowing there is money available if needed is very comforting. Savers are prepared for rainy days, although they hate to part with their money even then. Thrifty people in our society are treated with respect since they embody the solid citizen image. Thriftiness, after all, is a cherished value. There is no such thing as Cheapskates Anonymous!

The frugal are survivors. Periods of inflation, stock market crashes, and recessions don't bother them. They know how to stretch their dollars, where to shop for the best deals, and they don't complain if they live beneath their means. They're able to make do with what they have. When they shop, they spot the best deals and don't mind going out of their way to get them. They look at people who buy retail as fools.

Kids who come from penny-pinching homes may grow up with a limited supply of both money and demonstrated love. It's difficult to convey warmth in a chilly atmosphere where conserving energy can include hugs and kisses as well as finances, and priorities get misconstrued if kids think that by not spending they will earn some affection from their parents.

It's difficult to be secure in an environment where finding money to pay the bills each month is uppermost in everyone's mind. We are all insecure to some extent, but those who become excessively frugal have more insecurity and fear than others; consequently, they may spend their energy on buttressing themselves against misfortune and exploitation. Here are some examples:

Roy, who takes care of the house while his wife works, always tries to buy necessities with coupons or fix things instead of replacing them. He even recycles paper towels by hanging them up to dry on a little clothesline. If Roy and his wife go out for dinner, the restaurant must offer two-for-the-price-of-one dinners. He knows a bank that has free coffee and doughnuts, so Roy goes there for breakfast—every day.

Diana has enough shampoo and toilet paper for at least a year. Her husband can't understand why she spends so much money this way since they'll have to scrimp in other areas, but Diana cannot resist a good sale. Her husband, however, is used to a more even distribution of wealth and household supplies.

Brenda can't stand it when her husband, Rich, pinches pennies. "He'll turn off the car motor about half way up the street and coast into the driveway to save money on gas."

Roy, Diana, and Rich grew up with the knowledge that they were expected to save money. Their parents watched their nickels and dimes and conveyed repeatedly that money was not to be treated lightly. Diana remembers, "It was a fact of life that I had one pair of shoes for good and one for school. When the school shoes wore out, I got a new pair, but I had to wear the dress shoes until they were absolutely too tight for comfort. That's why I go ballistic when my kids bug me for new sneakers. They can't conceive of being uncomfortable."

Growing up in a home without much money can be constricting, if not downright painful. There are so many temptations and pressures around that the word *no* is very familiar. One teenager says, "I heard 'You can't have this or that' so often that I just gave up asking. To be honest, I really felt angry and jealous of the other kids who went to the movies and had great toys, but I learned to keep quiet about it."

Every three-year-old child knows how to ask for things. They assert themselves by pointing, pouting, and crying. They want everything. Over time, if their requests are not met, they may learn not to ask for anything and respond by becoming depressed or guilt-ridden.

Kids get depressed because they have to keep their feelings in. It's too dangerous to throw a tantrum or yell or scream. "Not only can't you have what you want, but you can't express how angry it makes you," said Josie. She went on to say, "My mother sent me to my room to punish me for letting the tears roll down my face when she said I couldn't get a new dress for my friend's sweet sixteen party. All I said was what I wanted, but I felt like a bad person just for asking. After sitting in that room as if in solitary confinement, I got real mad and cursed her out loud. She couldn't hear, but I felt guilty anyway."

GUILT

Guilt is frequently the punishment for nasty thoughts and feelings. *Should* and *shouldn't* usually indicate guilt too. "I shouldn't spend money on that," "I should save more," "I shouldn't feel envious," "I shouldn't ask, let alone desire" are the words that inner voice utters when the possibility of spending money comes up.

Many children are taught that self-indulgence is sinful. So many kids are admonished for their selfishness that they go through life not wanting, not asking, and not being aware of life's temptations. Therapists spend a considerable amount of time helping many of their clients differentiate between selfishness and self-centeredness.

Selfishness has been given a bad reputation. The real culprit is self-centeredness. Taking care of one's self is extremely important and has more to do with protection than indulgence. Self-centeredness is different. Here, the person acts and expects others to react as if he were the center of the universe. This is more than indulgence, it is infuriating. If only kids could be taught to be selfish and not self-centered, there would be less guilt and more relatedness. However, the admonition "Don't be selfish" still reigns and can lead to self-denial.

Self-deniers put on a brave front of "having everything they need, thank you." They engender guilt in others who appear to be gluttonous in their material tastes in contrast to them and their no-frills simplicity. They don't want others to feel envious toward them. They don't want to feel obligated to others, so they don't enjoy receiving gifts, but most of all, they want to avoid their own feelings of envy or anger. If they are self-sufficient, they can mind their own business, do without asking things of others, and even earn the admiration of others. By conveying, "Go ahead, have a good time. I'll watch," they stay aloof from what they consider financial wastefulness. In the meantime, everyone else questions whether they have a right to indulge.

DISCUSSING FRUGALITY
WITH KIDS

Talking about money, and the pattern of frugality in particular, opens up problem areas that can be corrected. If a child is feeling "poor," for example, a dose of reality is in order. Just how poor one really is needs to be spelled out. Does the child have to pinch pennies or can there be some extra discretionary money? Can the teen think of ways to earn some "fun" money if he admits he'd like to be with the gang? What are the assets, savings, and bills? What's the reality of the family budget? If the teen imagines a tighter financial situation than really exists some discussion can put the child on a looser track. *Poor* can be a frame of mind and have nothing to do with reality. If that's the case, you will have to dig deeper.

Lack of money can be a handy excuse for avoiding involvement with the other kids. The frugal teen can rationalize, "It's because I don't have money that they don't invite me," rather than, "They don't like me or they'd invite me."

Insecurity can also be discussed. If your teen feels she can't keep up with the other kids, find out the details. Are "all the kids" getting gigantic allowances, new clothes, and going places, or does it just seem that way, because the one or two kids your child wants to befriend are in the fast crowd? Help your child talk about the other kids' values and question those who equate being "in" with having money to spend. Talk about what she has to offer in a friendship.

Encourage your child to try to undo the notion that people will hurt her by urging her to meet new people. If she can find one person to be friends with, suggest how she could nudge the friendship along. The more positive experiences there are with people, the less the child will think that it's wise to avoid them. "Not everyone will hurt or disappoint you" is a balancing thought. The trick is to continue to risk rejection without taking it too hard if it occurs.

Talk about how to have fun without spending money or with very little money. It's fun to experiment with buying something impulsively just to see how it feels. If it feels good, try it again. When your child does the marketing, have him buy something extra for a change, such as a magazine, candy, or different fruits and vegetables. When a new season rolls around, suggest trying out a new color or a new style. Give your child permission to loosen up, and do so yourself.

How your child talks to himself can be improved. Emphasize being kind and nurturing and try to stop thinking thoughts such as, "I really don't need this," "I'll make do with what I have and wait until after-Christmas sales next year," "This isn't worth the money even though I like it," or "Too bad it's not on sale." Instead, learn to say, "It's okay to buy things I want every now and then," "I don't have to deprive myself to feel good," "Things don't have to last forever," and "If I can afford it, I can have it."

Since fears underly frugality, talking about what they are is a good antidote. Some of the worst fears would never come true. For example, if your child fears that there isn't enough money for college, he may think he can't go. That may be a faulty assumption. You may not have even realized that college was his goal. Talking will at least get some thoughts and feelings aired, and a game plan will evolve.

Some kids fear that they won't be able to succeed financially. They may feel overwhelmed by thoughts of a bleak future with few job prospects and less hope of doing better than prior generations. They need to be reassured that they don't have to be overwhelmed children. Rather, they have to be encouraged to tap their talents, develop, and market them. They can get the training they need to take good care of themselves, if they don't put themselves down and erode their own self-esteem. They can learn to overcome their fears and assert themselves.

Anything that can enhance kids' feelings about themselves is helpful. Perhaps starting a list of things she likes about herself and adding to it every chance she gets will help. If she keeps this list on a notecard in her wallet, she can pull it out when she needs it. Doing things such as painting a room or fixing a car help kids feel a sense of accomplishment at the same time that they are saving money.

Remember that praise is cheap, but valuable. If you say you're proud of your child, that can be the best therapy.

PARENTAL GUIDELINES FOR DEALING WITH EXCESSIVE FRUGALITY

- **Be aware of symptoms such as isolation, sadness, and little interest in entertainment.**

- **Discuss thoughts and feelings about spending money.**

- **Consider how realistic it is to beware of spending.**

- **Would earning extra money help?**

- **Find out how money affects your child's friendships.**

- **Encourage your child to experiment with new purchases.**

- **Explore your child's fears and insecurities.**

18

GAMBLING

"I WON BETWEEN TWO HUNDRED AND FOUR HUNDRED DOL-lars a week during the NBA season last year," said a seventeen-year-old student at a local high school. "Then I lost, but won back about fifteen hundred dollars. The problem is, once you lose a lot of money, you want to get it back, so you keep betting. As soon as you get even, you want to try for more. There's no end to it."

His friend chimed in, "At first I won a few times in a baseball pool. It was only a few dollars, but it was exciting. As I got to know the teams and the players more, I won more. When I won two hundred dollars it was the wildest thing that ever happened to me. Then I lost thirteen hundred dollars in one month during basketball season! My grades went down the tubes, since I only cared about getting that money back. My bookie threatened to break my bones if I didn't pay him. Instead of doing my homework

I'd study the sports pages and pray I'd win. I played a real long shot on two games with the end of my savings and I won, but it was the grossest time of my life."

Bobby is nearly eighteen and he's a compulsive gambler. He wanted some easy money and envisioned winning enough to get himself a car. He spent a lot of time and money betting on sports and going to Atlantic City casinos. He's in Gamblers Anonymous now, but for the past four years he denied that he had a problem. During that time, he lost a lot of money yet continued to bet on sporting events, hoping to make it back. He worked in a restaurant on the New Jersey shore and bet all his money at the casinos, even though he was underage. When he needed more money, he took an advance on his credit card or asked his bookmaker for a loan. At one point, he owed as much as four thousand dollars to the bookmaker and had many sleepless nights before telling his parents about his problem. They got the shock of their lives, paid his debt, and strongly encouraged him to go to Gamblers Anonymous. He didn't seek help that time around because he thought he could control himself and gamble "normally." He went on to win—and lose—bigger amounts, while his schoolwork continued to suffer. When he owed eight thousand dollars to his bookmaker and seriously considered forging some of his father's checks, he finally admitted he had a problem.

EARLIEST INFLUENCES

In their earliest days, babies feel they are the center of the universe. All of their needs are met, and others cater to their whims as if by magic. Gradually, they learn to accept that they must do things for themselves.

Many people, especially gamblers, want to reexperience the earliest feeling of being very special. These are people who yearn for attention and to feel important. They are frustrated people, but when they win, they reclaim their exalted status, if only for a little while.

There are some factors that could cut short the usual period where infants appropriately maintain a central position in the family. If a new child comes into the family, there will be less attention available. If there's death, divorce, or dissension, the mother-and-child relationship could be strained. A sudden change in a parent's attitude, such as believing that the child could do more for himself or could wait longer for gratification, can have a long-lasting effect too.

If there is too little or too much stimulation, a baby may respond by wanting action and excitement. The need for excitement causes hyperactivity, both physically and through fantasy. These babies start out in a restless way and don't develop the usual sensitivity to subtleties in life.

During the "terrible two's" period, children normally begin to become separate little people. They say no a lot to assert themselves. This irks many parents, who either don't know this is normal behavior or just don't like it. Parents may respond by punishing or hurting the child, while others refuse to let the child have choices and convey that only they know what's best for baby. When these types of parental behaviors occur, kids learn to doubt themselves. They don't learn what they want or think and consequently don't gain self-confidence. These children become impulsive. They seem to just grab at things without thinking. They will grow up seeking distractions and reacting to them, rather than being initiators of things that could bring about a sense of accomplishment or self-expression. Since they don't learn to do things that could bring self-esteem from their own efforts, they try to get the good feeling from outside sources.

Preschool children identify with superheroes. They want to feel big and strong too. As they battle their own wishes to be bad, the superheroes help them to triumph over these impulses. Most kids can accept the necessity to adjust to certain realities such as learning not to hit, bite, or take things that don't belong to them. In play and fantasy, they can be the good guys who go after those who don't behave properly. Play helps kids to integrate the lessons parents, teachers, and society demand of them. They will be loved for their efforts, and that's motivation enough to give up antisocial behavior.

Kids who take play too far are unable or unwilling to turn it off when the game ends. They use their imagination to revise reality. They confuse what is real with what is merely a wish. Storybook fantasies such as fairy tales encourage these children to believe in success stories. If make-believe characters can go from rags to riches, they might also. If entertainers and sports figures can make millions of dollars, maybe they can too, if they find the right way to do so. Gambling offers the chance of instant success, the hope of being the one with the magic beans or having the hen that lays golden eggs.

Eventually, these kids test their own luck by trying to get away with things. They'll steal something from a store or take some change from your wallet. If they aren't caught, they feel lucky, successful, and smart enough to beat the system. This is what passes as self-esteem and being special, so it will be repeated.

Children who grow up in homes where their parents watch their every move and are too punitive and powerful in their disciplinary tactics are made to feel weak, vulnerable, silly for even trying, and even incompetent. They grow up treating others punitively and themselves very liberally to offset the parents' ways with them. This results in frequent rewards and rationalizations. They permit themselves to do things that go beyond what is reasonable, and they go overboard in treating or consoling themselves, opening the gates for theft, drugs, alcohol, and gambling. That magical thinking of age five or six persists, so the child believes himself to be a success when no real sense of mastery or real accomplishment exists.

If the child does not do well in school, he's likely to want to hide that reality also. His sense of underachievement and depression go away when he lets his imagination loose. He feels he's not like everyone else and doesn't have to do what others do. Instead of working on projects that demand a process, he'll get things done at the last minute. He develops a certain charm that seduces teachers into being more gentle with him. He makes believable excuses and lives by his wits.

Understandably, he doesn't make many friends. He's limited in his ability to relate to others on anything but a superficial level. Later on, other gamblers provide a pseudo friendship when they hang out together and share each other's success stories.

A GROWING TEENAGE PROBLEM

An increasing number of teenagers gamble on a regular basis. Kids as young as twelve know how to gamble, and by the time they reach eighteen, signs of pathological gambling can appear. If they live near casinos, they are more apt to gamble even though they are underage, because if they're persistent, the casinos let them in.

In addition to sports and casino betting, teens play the lotteries that are now legal in just about every state. They bet on horses without much interference when they are accompanied by adults at the track. They play cards, dice, and bingo. Some kids use their lunch money for bets, others steal, some sell shoplifted items or drugs for money. As gambling becomes more socially acceptable in this country, teens are more apt to use their discretionary money for poker games, video games, and anything else they can bet on—even whether a teacher will assign homework.

The teen years are usually when a compulsive-gambling problem begins. In some schools, gambling is a bigger problem than drugs and alcohol. It's done surreptitiously at school, at parties on the weekends, and at home. Unlike substance abuse, this one has no physical symptoms. It is similar to other compulsive behaviors in that it is addictive, has a usual downward pattern, and is treatable in the right circumstances.

It's usually the boys who are smart, competitive, and good in math who like to gamble. Although they're able to watch TV sports for hours, they get bored and crave stimulation most of the time. They have a false front of bravado because, underneath, they feel very uncomfortable about themselves and can't cope with criticism or rejection. They usually come from troubled homes where there are many family problems. Alcohol, gambling, or workaholism may be part of the family life-style. Money may be overemphasized. Talk about taking risks in the stock market may be common. Divorce may be a factor. Attention is a scarce thing.

Deborah suspected that her son, Aaron, was gambling because he spent a lot of time switching channels for sports news on television and reading the newspapers for scores. He seemed obsessed with all sorts of sporting events. She noticed that Aaron was irritable much of the time and had trouble getting his schoolwork in on time, since he said he couldn't concentrate on it.

Her husband gambled at weekly card games where hundreds of dollars changed hands frequently. She knew from years of experience that gambling could be hazardous. It was more than once that she had to deal with creditors because her husband lost the household money at the card table.

The tension in the home was generally high, since so much rested on whether he'd win or lose. If Deborah's husband lost, he'd be morose and would demand that everyone at home be quiet and leave him alone. Sometimes he'd yell, and other times he'd watch television all day without getting dressed. When he won, he looked forward to going back for more. Paying bills was possible, but buying new furniture was out of the question since he needed his gambling money. Aaron subsequently felt he needed to contribute to the family budget and often justified his gambling as a way to make extra money to give to his mother.

While women gamble less, they frequently take their daughters with them when they play bingo or cards. Kids who want their parents' attention will learn to gamble. If they go to racetracks on family outings, they'll follow their parents' lead with betting.

If husbands are alcoholic or unavailable in other ways, wives might gamble to pass the time and numb some feelings. While gambling may start out as a way to add a little fun or to decrease some loneliness for teenagers, it can inadvertently teach them that working for money doesn't pay as much as a winning streak. Teens who can't or don't want to wait for future rewards see gambling as a shortcut. They can have what they want faster than the kids who work for minimum wage. Gambling is a means to buy some freedom to do one's own thing. It's a way out of a nine-to-five existence. There are no restrictions and no bosses. Gambling provides excitement and escape from daily troubles. Winning brings respect. Those benefits are hard to resist, especially if impulsivity is part of the personality.

The goals of gambling are to "make a killing," to "win big," to be a "big shot," to be "a winner." Those who get a lot of money without working for it feel smarter than the ordinary Joes who toil day in and day out for less gain and surely for less excitement. The lure of easy money is powerful.

Indeed, it is the excitement of being special, of having Dame Fortune smile on them, that makes people gamble. The "action" is so exciting that it can be addictive. Winning has been described as a "warm glow all over," "a coming alive," and as "being somebody." They especially love the power that comes with a filled wallet. People flock around a winner, and it's a heady feeling to be able to treat those who share the moment. People such as Diamond Jim Brady make their reputations by giving lavish gifts and tips to everyone. In return, they get deference, admiration, and the best table in restaurants. It seems they can have whatever they want, as long as they have plenty of money. Money substitutes for love and is a quick and efficient means to secure attention and power.

Many people who are alcoholics or substance abusers are also compulsive gamblers. They forget their troubles when they engage in these activities and feel good. That is why they have to repeat them. A large part of what they try to escape from has to do with low self-esteem and feelings of being a nobody.

Initially, winning is exciting and stimulates optimism about continuing success and being a big shot. After the initial period, occasional gambling leads to more frequent gambling with larger amounts of money. The wonderful feelings subside and the gambler gradually goes downhill and so does his job, family, and friendships. The gambler loses control of himself. The inability to pay debts causes him to lie, cover up, and become self-involved and alienated from others. The stress of "chasing" (continuing to bet to cover losses) can wreak havoc on family life. Bills may be unpaid, debts may pile up, crimes may even be committed for more money in order to "get even." Jobs are lost and so are reputations and marriages. Gambling, like other compulsions, becomes the focus of family life, not the kids. Instead, kids who get in the way or try for some attention are frequently rebuffed or abused. At worst, suicide results from the sense of hopelessness in the gambler.

WHAT TO DO

Children ought to know that gambling can become a dangerous pastime. If you suspect your child has a problem, look for these symptoms: underachievement at school, no friends, no hobbies, tendencies to get away with things, lying, actual trouble with the law, and a depressed mood. Any one of these symptoms would be cause for getting help, so a whole package truly indicates that the youth is in trouble.

You might also talk to your child's teacher to get a fuller picture of what goes on at school, especially whether his crowd has been caught or suspected of gambling. In most schools, gambling is an offense punishable by expulsion, and you need to alert your child to that possibility.

Of course, the best possible remedy for gambling or any vice begins early with adequate parenting, love, and attention. As for money, it becomes very important to kids around age eight, so that is a time to be especially careful how you handle it with them. If they have access to money by keeping the change from grocery shopping when you haven't okayed it, and by picking up spare change from dresser tops, they might view this as lucky and go on to look for more easy money. Don't let children get away with helping themselves to your change or wallet.

Plan activities or household chores that will give your child a sense of accomplishment and help build self-esteem.

Set some limits and stick to them consistently. When kids have problems with money, take away financial privileges and keep track of how much money they should have. Parents can also take away the allowance, credit cards, bank card, and checkbook, but only as a punishment for misusing money. Some parents pay off their teen's gambling debts without setting up a system for the teen to reimburse them, and this doesn't teach the teen anything except that he will be bailed out. By bailing out a teenage gambler, the behavior is "enabled," which means the parent becomes the culprit, too. The message you send is that the teen will be taken care of, and this further erodes the chance for the teen to grow responsibly. If a teen works, then some means of control is necessary to prevent him from using his money for gambling.

Kids who do "bad" things, such as gambling or stealing, sometimes do it to get some attention, even if that takes the form of a beating or other harsh punishment. Any attention is better than none. However, the cure is not in providing the needed love, it's in the teen's taking responsibility and control of himself, talking to a therapist, participating in a Twelve-Step program, learning how to relate to people, and finding better ways to feel good about himself.

When all else fails, seek help. If the gambling has spiraled downward to the point where it can no longer be denied as a problem, or if it's suspected as a problem, Gamblers Anonymous is the best place to seek help. This might occur only after numerous lies, bailouts, illegal acts, and emotional breakdowns occur, or when guilty and shameful feelings surface. Teens may feel uncomfortable at meetings, since most members are adults, but every effort must be made to encourage attendance nevertheless. Gam-Anon is for family members of gamblers and is necessary, since this is a family problem and each member is affected. Some psychotherapists who are trained to work with families can be very helpful. In localities where Gam-Anon is unavailable, other Twelve-Step programs such as Alcoholics Anonymous and Al-Anon can help. These self-help programs are effective as long as all members of the family participate regularly. Psychotherapy in conjunction with a self-help program can help gamblers best. They will know they are not alone in their despair. Treatment provides an opportunity to work out some of the social and psychological tasks that were neglected in the past.

PARENTAL GUIDELINES FOR DEALING WITH GAMBLING

- **Admit to having a problem.**

- **Discuss the effects gambling has on schoolwork, social life, and family functioning.**

- **Develop hobbies and interests.**

- **Recognize positive changes and reward them.**

- **Identify feelings that precede gambling sprees, put them into words, and begin to change the behavior.**

- **Seek help from Gamblers Anonymous and psychotherapy.**

CONCLUSION: PARENTS AS ROLE MODELS

HOW WAS MONEY HANDLED BY YOUR PARENTS? ASK A DOZEN people and you'll get a dozen different responses. The following are some common ones: "There were always fights over who got what or over how much things cost." "I got money pretty much when I asked for it." "In my family, it was feast or famine, so I never really knew if I'd get what I wanted." "When I got sick, I got more presents than for my birthday." "I'd ask my Dad for extra money since Mom was a cheapskate." "Mom made out the bills, but Dad made the decisions." "Nobody got anything without whining or carrying on."

Kids know who exerts power over money on a daily basis in their families. They learn who makes the decisions, pays the bills, saves, and squanders. They get messages about what men and women do with money, who holds the purse strings, and whether financial decisions are made jointly or independently. They feel the tension if Dad is threatened by Mom earning a paycheck or if there's not enough money to pay bills or taxes because of alcoholism or gambling.

Despite the number of child-rearing books, courses, and word-of-mouth advice available on the park bench and television talk shows, the most influential teachers are our own parents. Growing up and absorbing their rhythms, whims, and even limitations is par for the course until the time comes when questioning some or all of what they say or do becomes a priority to us. Many people hold onto behavioral patterns that may not be so terrific, because it's easier to be a copycat than to take the trouble to forge a new style.

Usually people repeat or rebel against what is familiar because the subtleties of in-between behavior don't seem to get them the responses they want. It has been said that imitation is the sincerest form of flattery, and, for some, there are great rewards from following in a parent's footsteps. If, on the other hand, it seems too dangerous to depend on or to be like the parent, the child will be exactly the opposite.

CONFLICTING STYLES

Totally different money styles within the same family are not uncommon, because spending is a way to assert one's differences. We must also remember that each child within the same family technically has different parents, since each child was born to people at changing times in life.

And, since opposites do attract, parents might also present conflicting role models to their children. Consider the case of Carl the Careful and Carla the Careless. Before they got married, they helped each other to enjoy life more. She persuaded him to loosen up and spend more money during weekends of dining and dancing at mountain resorts, and he tried to tighten her up by teaching her how to balance her checkbook.

After they got married, he spent long hours at the store he owned, and she spent money in stores she discovered on her lunch hour. The more attention he gave to business and the wish to be economically sound, the more resentful she felt, and the more purchases she made. Consequently, the amount of money spent was in proportion to the amount of attention she lacked. The higher the bills, the higher Carl's blood pressure went. The looser Carla was with money, the tighter Carl became. Indeed, the fights persisted and the needs of each remained ungratified.

Can you imagine being Carl and Carla's child? Whom do you imitate? Whom do you please? Can you go to one for small change and the other for big-ticket items? If Dad's feathers get ruffled with the sounds of requests for things, either the child will learn to not ask or she'll find other ways to get what she wants.

MONEY AS SECURITY

As we said earlier, adults who are excessively frugal may not have gotten enough love and money in childhood. They might also become supersavers, self-deniers, collectors, or extraordinary bargain hunters. They use money to fend off feelings of insecurity.

On the dark side of insecurity lurks suspiciousness and out-and-out paranoia. It must be uncomfortable to imagine everyone as a thief who is out to rip you off or take advantage of you in some way. Holding onto money is the only security these fearful types know. Parents who exhibit this behavior will pass along their fearfulness to their children as well.

MONEY AS LOVE

Unfortunately, many children grow up without experiencing any parental approval, pride, or demonstrated love. They wonder if they are lovable, worthy, or deserving. There's an inner emptiness they try to fill with possessions. These are the people who give big tips to get smiles, which they equate with love. They tend to be generous with gifts so they can feel appreciated.

Money can be the means to get rid of difficult, uncomfortable feelings such as frustration, depression, restlessness, and downright rage. People buy comfort foods such as doughnuts, chocolate cake, and ice cream to feed and soothe the angry beast inside that feels so upset. Millions of dollars are spent on movies and other forms of entertainment to take our mind off our troubles. Lots of people buy drugs and alcohol to feel better. Many treat themselves to days off or compensate for some form of emotional neglect by stealing yellow pads, pens, and other valuables from work when they feel unrewarded there. When children watch their parents act this way, they will repeat the process or choose an inappropriate method of coping all their own.

Kids see the look of pride on their parents' faces when they show off their possessions. It's when possessions are substitutes for feeling good inside that they become temporary solutions to a chronic problem. Instead of buying to demonstrate high performance, it's more important to feel self-confidence in one's own abilities and accomplishments.

Hugs and kisses do more to raise children's self-esteem than all the things combined in their toy chests. There is no price for the glint in a mother's eye, which is the parental seal of approval. Firm feelings of being worthwhile and lovable are also priceless. To feel this way as adults, however, we must experience our worthiness and lovability over and over as children. For the adults who confuse money with love, there were probably more pleasurable experiences with things than with people when they were kids.

MONEY AND POWER

When money is a symbol of power, the way is open to abusing money instead of using it. The power seekers come from backgrounds where there was a great deal of pain. They never want to feel powerless, humiliated, or out of control. Whether through abuse, alcoholism, prejudice, divorce, rejection, or some other major long-standing hurtful pattern, the growing child vows to never, ever, experience it again, or he'll do to others what was done to him. To guard against the most uncomfortable feelings of vulnerability, weakness, and powerlessness, the power seeker will resort to intimidation and rage to keep others in line. Consequently, to maintain a relationship with a power seeker, one must follow orders, be submissive, and be willing to please.

The power people tend to marry dependent sorts who like to be behind the scenes and reflect the power and glory. There's no power struggle if one is always right or is the decision maker and the other goes along without complaint. There are no arguments when it's okay for one to be in charge of the financial affairs, and the other doesn't question the routine. Problems crop up when family members want to become more independent and fulfill themselves, get educated, or start working to have money of their own.

Many children who grow up in homes where money is used as power eventually "do unto others what was done to them." They know it's better to be the one in control, instead of the one who is weak and vulnerable. Since they have experienced the humiliating feelings of being powerless, their anger lies just beneath the surface, and they don't hesitate to intimidate others in order to keep them in line. Leaders of industry and politicians appear to seek power through wheeling and dealing, but maybe they are actually protecting themselves from the uncomfortable feelings they experienced when they were young.

There are some children who rebel against the power of money. They don't want to compete, take risks, or join the rat race. Rather, they want to be out of this loop altogether, and they often cop out with drugs or alcohol.

In a way, this is their form of "kid power." By being bad and getting attention in negative ways, these children clearly say, "You'll pay for this!" Major problems such as drug abuse, eating disorders, gambling, and excessive spending are also products of this message. These children don't want to compete as their parents do. They don't want to be what their parents expect them to be. Some get depressed and even kill themselves trying to exert some power of their own, albeit in highly destructive ways. Parents who are power mongers might consider whether they are able to empower their children more, to prevent these destructive behaviors.

Money is also frequently held out as a reward or punishment and as a common means of exerting control. Most parents will try to control their kids with money at some time, but this is especially true of power seekers.

The whole concept of "if you do what I want you to, then I'll give you a monetary prize" needs some examination. Doing well in school, for example, is what a child ought to be doing to satisfy his own expectations and to feel good about himself. There are inner values that are more enduring to be gained from improving one's grades or studying harder. If money is given for school performance, then the child learns more about satisfying someone else's agenda then making his own.

The child who sets his own sights on improving his grades will focus more on the process than on the end result. Study habits and self-discipline are parts of the process that get taken for granted if the grade becomes the sole determiner of success. The love of learning for its own sake gets lost too, if only the final grade is emphasized. Offering money for good grades is really a bribe which says to the child, "*If* you do this, you'll get this."

Bribes, in general, are manipulative and don't work in the long run.

Kids need parental approval and want to please, but we don't want them to cheat or compromise their integrity to get the scores on tests and papers, and offering a bribe will do this. Encouragement and empathy help kids make good grades, and they get lasting memories too of parental kindness. That's more important than trying to motivate kids by dangling money, television sets, or a car in front of them. Life isn't a game show where prizes are given for answering questions correctly.

When kids continually have to ask for money, they are put into a dependent position. They have to depend on the parent not only for the money but for agreeing that the money is necessary. The child will think twice about whether to ask, especially if the history of asking was that of rejection. The parent who controls the purse strings risks resentment from children who are put into this position. It is much better to set the allowance as presented in the previous chapters and then offer "bonuses" and "matched funds" which are clearly defined for your child.

Let them know if there will be extra money for them for certain chores, and they will want to go the extra mile to take on these tasks because there is something in it for them. Their attitude will be positive because, instead of feeling submissive, they have control over whether they want to take on the task in the first place. They'll even ask what they can do for extra money, since by giving them choices, you empower them and eliminate hard feelings as well as nagging.

Money should never be used as a disciplinary tool. Withdrawing privileges or stating your disapproval or disappointment are better methods of motivating your child to follow the rules or improve behavior. These methods will also not act as negative influences on your child in later years, whereas withholding money, especially the allowance, can and will.

Of course, parents want to instill respect for property in kids, yet is it realistic to penalize kids by withholding their allowance to make the point? What if something truly valuable breaks, such as memorabilia or fine art—can you hold a child financially responsible? Remorse and repentance are of utmost importance. Accidents do happen, after all. If asked, kids can come up with their own plan of showing they're sorry too.

YOUR OWN INFLUENCES

While there are plenty of outside sources of stimulation, such as television and peer pressure, the cues children pick up from their parents regarding money are the most influential. The feelings experienced by a child at home will be powerful guides for determining her own money style, with everything from joy to resentment possible. When a child gets what he wants, he is usually pleased, and when he doesn't, he feels bad. A pattern of repeated feelings is what teaches the child attitudes toward money.

It can be very helpful to see how your own attitudes were formed. Let your mind wander back to your childhood as you answer the following questions. The memories that surface can help you understand what your parents taught you about money. There are no right or wrong answers. This is just an exercise to stimulate some thoughts and, it is hoped, conversation. By reexperiencing some feelings stirred up by the questions, you'll have a chance to know how your own child might feel in similar circumstances. Perhaps you can change some of the ways you're teaching your child if you feel uncomfortable repeating things that were not successful when you grew up.

YES	NO	
_____	_____	Were you able to have most of what you wanted as a child?
_____	_____	Did you feel all right about asking for things?
_____	_____	Was your family financially comfortable?
_____	_____	Were your friends better off than you?
_____	_____	Were you taught enough about money to manage it confidently?
_____	_____	Was your allowance adequate?
_____	_____	Did your parents argue about money?
_____	_____	Did outside events affect your family's finances?
_____	_____	Was money a means of control in your family?
_____	_____	Were you told to have fun with money?
_____	_____	Was either of your parents too loose or too tight with money?
_____	_____	Are you like one of your parents in how you handle money?

————— ————— Do you worry about money matters?
————— ————— Were you encouraged to earn extra money?

Use these questions as a guideline for teaching your own child the financial facts of life. And remember, it's never too early—or too late—to help your child profit from the proper appreciation and use of money.

BIBLIOGRAPHY

Altfest, Lewis J., and Altfest, Karen Caplan. *Lew Altfest Answers Almost All Your Questions about Money.* New York: McGraw-Hill, 1992.

Angier, Natalie. "Fear of Finance." *Mademoiselle*, January 1989, pp. 150–151.

Arnott, Nancy. "Hey, Little Spender." *American Baby*, January 1991, p. 34

Baldwin, Bruce A. "Externalized Self-Esteem: A Growing Problem for Children." *Piedmont Airlines*, September 1987, pp. 15–19.

———. "Marital Materialism." *US Air Magazine*, April 1991, pp. 76–86.

Barbanel, Linda. "Guilt and Money." *Parents League Review*, 20 (1986): 240–244.

———. "Piggy-Bank Savvy." *Essence*, May 1986, p. 16.

———. "Children and Money." *ParentGuide News*, December 1986, p. 10.

———. "Giving a Child an Allowance: Learning Money Lessons—and More." *The Big Apple Parents' Paper*, September 1988, p. 18.

———. "How to Handle Money." *ParentGuide News*, December 1988, p. 20.

———. *Fifty Favorite Questions about Kids and Money.* New York: Linda Barbanel, 1989.

———. "Make His Day." *The Women's Record*, June 1989, p. 21.

———. "Kids & Money." *New York Family*, August 1991, p. 32.

———. "Kids & Money." *The Women's Record*, January 1992, p. 22.

———. "Helping Teens to Manage Money." *Our Town*, 16 January 1992, p. 17.

Beckman, Judith. "Fiscal Fitness." *The Women's Record*, May 1989, p. 10–11.

———. "Best Deals Around in Sound." *Zillions, Consumer Reports for Kids*, October/November 1990, pp. 10–13.

———. "A Cost-Containment Christmas." *New York Newsday*, 30 November 1991, p. 1.

Bishop, Pete. "Moms, Dads, Kids & Money." *The Pittsburgh Press*, 21 December 1990, pp. D1–D2.

Bjorklund, David, and Bjorklund, Barbara. "Children and Money." *Parents*, April 1987, p. 202.

———. "Born to Shop." *Extra Credit, Scholastic Inc.*, November 1991, pp. 20–22.

Brenner, Lynn. "Hope Your Kid Matures When His Bonds Do." *Newsday*, 20 May 1990, p. 28.

Briles, Judith. *The Dollars and Sense of Divorce*. New York: MasterMedia Limited, 1988.

Brown, Kathy. "Smallest Consumers Are Biggest Surprise." *Adweek*, 2 March 1992, p. 6.

Byers, Patricia; Preston, Julia; and Johnson, Patricia. *The Kids' Money Book*: *Great Money Making Ideas*. Maryland: Liberty Publishing Co., 1983.

Cantarella, Marcia. "Dear Marcia." *The Big Apple Parents' Paper*, December 1986, p. 22.

Castro, Janice. "The Simple Life." *Time*, 8 April 1991, pp. 58–65.

Celis, William, 3d. "Lessons about Business and Hard Times as Well." *New York Times*, 19 March 1992, p. 5.

Clifford, Jane. "Teaching Young Spenders to Save." *Brooklyn Journal*, 10–16 January 1991, p. 18.

Colino, Stacey. "Making Allowances Work." *American Health*, October 1990, p. 78.

Cook, James R. *The Start-Up Entrepreneur*. New York: Perennial Library, 1986.

Copeland, Jeff, and de Moraes, Lisa. "How to Teach Your Kids about Money." *Parenting*, March 1989, p. 45.

Crocker, David; Forbat, Pamela Savage; and Pike, Elizabeth. "Kid Counselor." *Registered Representative*, September 1989, pp. 16–20.

Davies, Gerry. "People with No Game Plan Also Have No Savings Plan." *American Banker*, 4 September 1987, p. 16.

Davis, W. Allison, and Havighurst, Robert J. *Father of the Man*. Boston: Houghton Mifflin, 1947.

Davis, Ken, and Taylor, Tom. *Kids and Cash*: *Solving a Parents' Dilemma*. La Jolla: Oak Tree Publications, 1979.

Dranov, Paula. "Do Cash and Chum-ship Mesh?" *Cosmopolitan*, October 1988, pp. 233–235.

Easton, Nina. "Americans Find Little Lure in Saving for a Rainy Day." *American Banker*, 4 September 1987, pp. 7–8.

Elkind, David. *The Hurried Child*: *Growing Up Too Fast Too Soon*. New York: Addison Wesley, 1981.

Estess, Patricia. "Should You Lend Money to a Relative? When to Say 'Yes' and How to Say 'No'." *Parade Magazine*, 24 July 1988, pp. 4–5.

Estess, Patricia, and Rosenthal, Lois. "Kids and Money." *Sylvia Porter's Personal Finance*, July/August 1988, pp. 32–36.

Farnham, Margaret. "Compulsive Spenders." *The Toledo Blade*, 26 April 1987, p. 1F.

Finkle, David. "Sticky Fingers." *New York Woman*, July/August 1987, pp. 61–63.

Flanagan, Patrick. "A Shy Shopper's Guide to Bargaining." *Self,* December 1985, pp. 48–50.

Fraiberg, Selma. *The Magic Years.* New York: Scribner's, 1959.

Fuller, Charles. "Now You Tee It (Now You Don't)." *Entrepreneur,* March 1992, p. 69.

Gesell, Arnold; Ames, Louise Bates; and Ilg, Frances L. *The Child from Five to Ten.* New York: Harper & Row, 1977.

"Give Yourself Some Credit." College Fund-Amentals, vol. 1, no. 1, 1991– 92, 4b–5b (Master Card International).

Godfrey, Neale S. *The Kids' Money Book.* New York: Checkerboard Press, 1991.

Goldberg, Herb, and Lewis, Robert T. *Money Madness.* New York: William Morrow and Company, 1978.

Goldinger, Jay. "Fiscal Education." *US Air,* September 1988, pp. 28–33.

Gosman, Fred G. *Spoiled Rotten: American Children and How to Change Them.* Milwaukee: Bashford & O'Neill, 1990.

Gould, Carole. "Where Prospectuses Fall Short." *New York Times,* 22 September 1991, p. 16F.

Hall, Trish. "Younger Consumers: More to Spend, More to Want." *New York Times,* 23 August 1990, p. C1.

Harris, Joan. "How to Help Your Graduating Son or Daughter Get That First Job." *The Women's Record,* April 1992, pp. 19–20.

Harris, Marlys J. "Save Now. Pay Later." *Parenting,* February 1989, p. 33.

———. "Teaching Your Children about Money." *Cleveland Jewish News,* 10 July 1992, p. 24.

Hathaway, Nancy Berman. "Fear of Buying: Women Who Save Too Much." *Harper's Bazaar,* January 1989, p. 38.

Hemp, Paul. "Saving—A Matter of Psychology." *New York Times,* 20 May 1984, p. 41.

Hinchcliff, Dorothy. "School Savings Programs Arousing New Interest." *American Banker,* 4 September 1987, p. 13.

Hodge, Marie. "When Giving (Cash) Is Better Than Receiving." *New Choices,* December 1988, p. 77.

———. "Teach Your Kids about Money." *Reader's Digest,* January 1989, pp. 54–58.

Houser, Peggy, and Hassell, Bradley. "How to Survive the Electronics Jungle." *Penny Power,* December 1988/January 1989, pp. 10–13.

How to Teach Children about Money. Denver: Western Freelance Writing Services, 1989.

"How to Make Money Collecting Coins." MCMLXXXV Mail Order Associates, Inc. Distributed by D. L. Leigh Enterprises, Michigan: 1992.

"How to Make Money Collecting Stamps." MCMLXXXV Mail Order Associates, Inc. Distributed by D. L. Leigh Enterprises, Michigan: 1992.

Huffman, Frances. "Small Wonders." *Entrepreneur*, March 1992, pp. 123–125.

Jacoby, Susan. "Compulsive Shopping." *Glamour*, April 1986, p. 318.

———. "Talking $$$ with Kids." *Family Circle*, 17 October 1989, p. 47.

Johnson, Rhonda. "Journey Through a Stock Exchange." New York: American Stock Exchange, 1988.

———. "These Parents Challenged Their Kids to Invest on Their Own." *Money*, March 1990, p. 128.

Karp, Abby. "Youths Gain Clout as Wage Earners, Consumers." *Baltimore Sun*, 8 October 1989, p. 1A.

Kelley, Bill. "Marketers Go Back to School." *Sales & Marketing Management*, November 1991, pp. 58–66.

Kindel, Sharen. "They May Be Small, but They Spend Big." *Adweek*, 10 February 1992, p. 4.

Kutner, Laurence. "You Can Indulge Children as Long as Some Limits Are Set." *New York Times*, 4 January 1990, p. C11.

———. "When Children Steal, Parents Should Know Why." *New York Times*, 10 September 1992, p. C12.

Kyte, Kathy S. *The Kids' Complete Guide to Money*. New York: Knopf, 1984.

Landau, Elayne. *The Smart Spending Guide for Teens*. New York: Simon & Schuster, Julian Messner, 1982.

Lesieur, Henry R. *Understanding Compulsive Gambling*. Center City, Minnesota: Hazelden, 1986.

Lorenz, Valerie C. "Differences Found among Catholic, Protestant and Jewish Families of Pathological Gamblers." Paper read at 5th National Conference on Gambling and Risk Taking, October 1981, Lake Tahoe, Nevada.

———. "Family Dynamics of Pathological Gamblers." In *The Handbook of Pathological Gambling*, edited by T. Galski, pp. 71–87. Springfield, IL: Charles C. Thomas, 1985.

Lorenz, Valerie C., and Yaffee, Robert A. "Pathological Gambling: Psychosomatic, Emotional and Marital Difficulties as Reported by the Spouse." *The Journal of Gambling Behavior* (Spring 1988): pp. 13–25.

McNeal, James U. "Shopping Is Child's Play." *Food & Beverage Marketing*, October 1989, p. 5.

McNeal, James U. " 'Little' Consumers Influence Spending Decisions." *Discount Store News*, 5 August 1991, pp. 78–80.

McNeal, James U. "The Littlest Shoppers." *American Demographics*, February 1992, pp. 48–53.

McNeal, James U. *A Handbook of Marketing to Children.* New York: Lexington Books, 1992.

Moe, Harold, and Moe, Sandy. *Teach Your Child the Value of Money.* Holmen, WI: Harsand Financial Press, 1990.

Moore, Lisa J. "The Littlest Consumers." *U.S. News & World Report,* 5 November 1990, pp. 73–75.

Osbim, Bob. "PEZ, anyone?" *Alabama Times Daily,* 27 February 1992, p. 7B.

Pike, Elizabeth. "Tackling Sell Signs." *Personal Investor,* July 1989, pp. 48–50.

Posluns, Ronald J. *Negotiate Your Way to Financial Success.* New York: Putnam, 1987.

Pousner, Michael. "Women Who Shoplift." *Cosmopolitan,* April 1988, pp. 162–171.

Rosen, Jan. "Teaching Youth Virtue of Saving." *New York Times,* 4 May 1991, p. 34.

Rosen, Marjorie D. "Teens and Money." *Ladies' Home Journal,* September 1991, p. 138.

Rosenthal, Richard J. "Pathological Gambling." *Psychiatric Annals* 22 (February 1992): 72–77.

Rowland, Mary. *The Fidelity Guide to Mutual Funds.* New York: Simon & Schuster, 1990.

———. "Teaching the Kids about Money." *New York Times,* 16 January 1991, p. D8.

———. "Fending Off the Season's Blues." *New York Times,* 1 December 1991, p. D8.

———. "Summer Businesses for Children." *New York Times,* 31 May 1992 p. D8.

———. "Business Cycles as a Board Game." *New York Times,* 9 August 1992, p. D8.

Sanger, Sirgay. "Prevention: Key to Youth Gambling Addiction—Part 1." *The National Council on Compulsive Gambling Newsletter* (November 1980), pp. 1–3.

———. "Prevention: Key to Youth Gambling Addiction—Part 2." *The National Council on Compulsive Gambling Newsletter* (May 1981), p. 5.

Schiffres, Manuel. "Getting Started in Stocks." *Kiplinger's Personal Finance Magazine,* July 1991, pp. 51–56.

Schifrin, Daniel. "Big Deal." *Baltimore Jewish Times,* 24 April 1992, pp. 54–57.

Schneider, Susan. "The Trade in Sticky Fingers." *Lear's,* September 1990, pp. 38–40.

Shapiro, Laura; Hager, Mary; and Denworth, Lydia. "Labels We Can Live By." *Newsweek*, 18 November 1991, p. 90.

"The Story of Checks and Electronic Payments." New York: Public Information Department, Federal Reserve Bank of New York, 1987.

"Kids & Money." *Ladies' Home Journal*, April 1989, p. 94.

Thornton, James. "Girls Who Steal." *Seventeen*, May 1992, pp. 86–87.

Toufexis, Anastasia. "365 Shopping Days Till Christmas." *Time*, 26 December 1988, p. 82.

Tumposky, Ellen. "Teaching the Value of a Dollar." *Daily News*, 11 August 1985, p. 6.

Weinstein, Grace W. *Children and Money: A Guide for Parents*. New York: Charterhouse, 1975.

INDEX

About the Author

Linda Barbanel, M.S.W, C.S.W, is a psychotherapist in private practice in New York City. In addition to treating individuals, she does marriage and couples' counseling and divorce mediation. She is a popular speaker and a frequent media guest on radio and television shows. Her comments on a multitude of psychological topics are quoted in more than 700 national publications, and her own articles appear in many as well. She is on the faculty of New York University, where she teaches courses on the "psychology of women and money."